D1394666

SEDIMENT

CJ: Charles Jennings is a writer and journalist whose books range from the best-selling travelogue *Up North*, to the state-of-the-union satire *Faintheart*, to the critically acclaimed *Them and Us* – a study of the American invasion of Edwardian high society. He has written for the *Daily Telegraph*, *Observer*, *Financial Times*, *Independent*, and *Esquire* magazine; and has been a columnist for the *Guardian* and *Times* newspapers. In between these jobs, he has written drama for Radio 4, presented *The Property Show* for Thames Televison, and, indeed, co-founded the wine blog, *Sediment*. He is currently a visiting Fellow at Goldsmiths College.

Married, with two sons, he lives in South-West London, where for relaxation he drinks wine costing not more than £5.99 a bottle.

PK: Paul Keers is a writer and magazine editor, whose articles have been published in more than thirty newspapers and magazines, from *Cosmopolitan* to the *Sunday Times*, and from the *Daily Mail* to the *FT Weekend*. He was the Launch Editor of *GQ* magazine in the UK, and his book, *A Gentleman's Wardrobe*, was published in four international editions. He also launched and ran a contract publishing agency, which published magazines for corporate clients including Conran, Guinness and the NCT. He is now an editorial consultant, and is co-founder of the wine blog *Sediment*.

He lives in West London, where his wife and their sons suffer his continuing delusion that wine will bring sophistication into their life.

SEDIMENT

Two Gentlemen and Their Mid-Life *Terroirs*

CJ and PK

JB

JOHN BLAKE

Published by John Blake Publishing Ltd,
3 Bramber Court, 2 Bramber Road,
London W14 9PB, England

www.johnblakepublishing.co.uk

www.facebook.com/johnblakebooks ⬜
twitter.com/jblakebooks ⬜

First published in hardback in 2014

ISBN: 978-1-78418-021-8

British Library Cataloguing-in-Publication Data:

A catalogue record for this book is available from the British Library.

Design by www.envydesign.co.uk

Printed in Great Britain by CPI Group (UK) Ltd, Croydon, CR0 4YY

1 3 5 7 9 10 8 6 4 2

Papers used by John Blake Publishing are natural, recyclable products made
from wood grown in sustainable forests. The manufacturing processes
conform to the environmental regulations of the country of origin.

Every attempt has been made to contact the relevant copyright-holders,
but some were unobtainable. We would be grateful if the appropriate
people could contact us.

Contents

Introduction

It was a couple of years ago. We were having lunch in a pizza restaurant. We were also drinking a bafflingly described, boldly overpriced and completely mediocre red: our normal wine consumption.

'This is appalling,' one of us said. 'Shall we have another bottle?'

The second bottle arrived, and the other one of us asked, 'Why does nobody write about these wines? Why do they only write about the good stuff? Someone should write a blog about real everyday wine drinking and real everyday wine, like this horrible Valpolicella.'

We thought this was such a good idea that we went ahead and did it. After all, we know more about writing than we do about wine, and we know more about wine than pizza. Which made it the perfect fit: *Sediment* was born.

The duties were unevenly divided from the start. Paul Keers (PK), a man who sees wine as a gateway to sophistication, connoisseurship and worldliness, a man who broods on social rituals, dinner guests and daunting wine merchants – a man who uses the word *etiquette* without irony – got the smarter end.

Charles Jennings (CJ), being a cheapskate *and* extremely credulous, believes, like a French *bourgeois*, that a casual, everyday enjoyment of wine at casual, absolutely rock-bottom prices, is every man's birthright. So he got all the rest.

That's how it is. Every week on the *Sediment* blog we wander along the pain threshold of wine drinking, never knowing enough, or spending enough, to get things right. It would be easy to say that the pleasure of the wine itself makes up for our tribulations. It would also be untrue. We've suffered – *really* suffered – as a consequence of our motto: 'I've bought it, so I'll drink it.'

This book is a collection of some of our best, but more often our worst, moments in wine. We hope you enjoy them more than we did.

CJ AND PK, AUGUST 2014

I
Buying It

Pounds and Pennies

PK

Take care of the pennies, they say, and the pounds will take care of themselves. Well, not when it comes to wine.

Down at the bottom of the wine lists, it seems that every bottle is now priced at something + 99p. From the murky depths where CJ unearths bottles for £3.99, to the wines for £10.99 and more which I find up at the snorkelling level.

And I'm forced to wonder why, in this age of electronic payment, the handing back of a penny in change persists – and whether I would feel better about my wine given a tiny, one penny rise in the price of a bottle, in order to round the prices up.

Some people assume that the reason for such prices is psychological – that we read from left to right, encounter the pounds figure first, and have registered the fact that it's, say, £7 + something, before we recalculate for the fact that the 'something' is actually nearly another whole pound. In our minds, we still think it's essentially a £7 bottle, not an £8 one.

But in fact, the origin of such pricing lay in forcing sales assistants to put cash from customers through the tills. By requiring staff to give change on every cash sale, it meant that they had to open the till, recording the transaction, and thereby reducing the opportunities for simply pocketing the customers' banknotes.

If I had a penny for every time someone has told me that, I'd have . . . well, I'd certainly have a penny.

Take care of the pennies? Personally, I don't want to take care of very many of them. A pocketful of pennies won't even buy you a newspaper; it will just spoil the line and damage the pockets of your suit. And sometimes you can't even give them away. I saw a chap once try to bestow a handful upon a Mancunian, but the latter was more interested in taking a corner kick at the time.

Be all that as it may; my concern here is with the pennies in the prices of wine. I once mocked a posh London wine merchant that was selling a bottle of La Mission Haut-Brion for £600.01. I just loved the idea of a City boy thumbing his wad, handing over a dozen £50 notes, and then scrabbling in his pockets for an additional penny. They did apologise, saying it was a computerised price-rise error; but the same merchants are currently selling a magnum of Bollinger Rosé NV champagne for £99.99.

Now let's be honest. If you handed over a brace of fifties for a bottle of Bolly, and got a penny back in change, would you exit the store, whistling gaily at your financial acumen? I think not.

In fact, I think exactly the opposite – you want to feel, and indeed would probably say to anyone who asked, that this was a Hundred-Pound Bottle of Champagne.

There seems to be a point, in most merchants' lists, at which prices switch, from .95 or .99, to round pounds. That point will differ from merchant to merchant – but that is often also the point, for them and for me, at which wine becomes Fine Wine.

At Majestic, for example, it seems to be £20. Below that, prices range from £4.99 to £19.99; then suddenly, magically, it's £22, £25, etc. And it works, on susceptible types like me.

Immediately, it's as if the wines have moved out of the bargains, and into a better class.

That's because small change has always been a bit . . . low rent. At the gentlemen's club Boodle's until quite recently they used to boil the coins given in change; silver used to be regarded as a notoriously unhygienic metal, due to its more frequent contact with the lower classes. Silver could not be considered as correct tender from one gentleman to another. And supposedly a vestige of this survives when a shop assistant, apologising for giving you change, says, 'Sorry it's all silver . . .'

But St James's isn't what it was. Berry Bros & Rudd, my benchmark for wine poshness, don't bother with pennies; their wines are priced to the nearest 5p; £7.95 rather than £7.99. But that goes right up to a bottle of L'Ermita 2006, at £427.90. Don't forget to pick up that 10p change, will you?

And then, insanely, they ask for a few paltry pennies on top of their case prices. So at the time of writing, twelve bottles of, say, Calon-Ségur 1996, is £1,064.16. That's well over a thousand pounds . . . plus 16p. And right at the very, very top of their list, they had a case of six magnums of La Tâche 1971. It's £25,000 a bottle (yes, that's twenty-five *thousand* pounds, a *very* gentlemanly sum) – but, for the case of six, it's £134,307 . . . *and 36p*. Where is the sophistication in spending the price of a small house on wine, and then quibbling about 36p? A bag of crisps with your drink, sir?

But we no longer live in a gentlemanly age. Wine prices, with their percentages of duty, VAT and margin, are presumably calculated by computer, resulting in the absurdities above. And we invariably pay by card, so the assistant only has to tap in four digits, be they 1499 or 1500, and has no need to consider any of the physical aspects of coins versus notes.

Nevertheless, I would feel less of a bargain hunter, and more of a gentleman, if that single penny were added to the price of a bottle. A £15 bottle of claret has more ring to it than one at £14.99. Whether or not it tastes like a Fine Wine, it *feels* more like one.

I would like a Hundred-Pound Bottle of Champagne, please. And not a penny less.

Ordering Online –
Tesco Cava

CJ

Well, the wife had the bright idea of ordering a load of cheap fizz in time for Christmas in order to keep the family lightly gassed throughout the nightmare we know as the Festive Period.

She found some Tesco Cava Brut going for a fantastic around-£4-a-bottle special online deal and ordered two cases. Then the snow fell and the UK came to a halt, all of our booze with it. No one knew where it was, not us, not Tesco. It might have been marooned in a delivery hub in Warrington, possibly not. Christmas edged nearer, no drink; Tesco promised pitifully that it would arrive in time for Christmas Eve. Christmas Eve came and went, as did Christmas Day, Boxing Day and the New Year holiday. Nothing.

Our grog finally turned up, quite unexpectedly, in mid-January. Good news was that they delivered vastly more than we'd asked for, presumably as an apology. *No no*, we cried as the light was blotted out by mountains of cardboard boxes, *some mistake*, but the delivery guys just shrugged and heaped the cases up in the hallway. Not only that, but Tesco threw in some fancier cavas (Cordoníu and Marques de Monistrol, 2006 vintage), I assume because they'd run out of the rock-bottom stuff we'd actually ordered.

Bad news too, because of course by mid-January everyone had checked into rehab to get over Christmas, and there was no possibility of our even beginning to drain the cava lake that had suddenly welled up in our lives. Moreover, it is now the end of March, and we still have thirty-two bottles to get through, and with the best will in the world, I am starting to struggle.

Not that there's anything wrong with the basic Tesco Cava, as long as you chill it to death. I know a guy who once worked with the Freixenet company and he was told (by the boss, indeed) that the way to serve cava was to chill it so much that ice crystals formed in the glass as you poured it. Which is terrific if you're in, say, Madrid, on a hot June night, less so in England in winter. Still, after some trial and error, my routine is to get the Tesco product down to a hairsbreadth above absolute zero, and what do I find but a nice prickly *mousse*, followed by a hint of burnt caramel on the tongue, then a ferocious *poof* as it expands rapidly across the floor of the mouth like a CO_2 fire extinguisher, leaving only a chesty rasp in its wake. It passes the time very nicely, especially when you consider what we paid.

Then I get bored. I still have over thirty bottles to get through, and how long does this stuff keep? PK suggests six months, but that's counting from January, which means I now have four months in which to neck my thirty bottles, which is roughly two bottles a week, and even with help from the wife and anyone else around, I don't think I have that much frivolity in me. So I try to trick myself into thinking the Tesco Cava is something else, not cava, by adding things to it.

Not the home-made sloe gin which No. 1 son once used to

make an intriguing champagne cocktail, only to discover that it produced a lethal fizzy syrup, a kind of psycho cherryade. No, I have professional kit, charitably donated in second-hand form by our French friends, in the shape of an almost-empty bottle of cassis; some Crème de Figue, similarly used; and a bottle of Crème de Pêche, almost untouched, which should have told me something.

As it turns out, the cassis is the only one I can look forward to without apprehension. It may have gone a bit brown in colour and have a certain amount of jammy horror around the neck, but Tesco Cava + elderly cassis = quite a funky sensation of cloves and gravy browning, oddly warming in the context of the frigid cava. The Figue, by way of contrast, while starting off with a promising chocolaty introduction, turns fairly quickly into a garbled story of deodorant, granulated sugar and aircraft dope. I want to like it, being the nearest in character to that slinky Crème de Noisette you sometimes find, but is it an inferior brand? Inherent nastiness? Something morbid turns the Figue into a drink occupying the narrow isthmus that connects the unusual to the merely weird, and I cannot bring myself to love it.

But at least it's not the Crème de Pêche. Peaches are lovely things. The label alone enchants. So why has it been barely touched? Well, as it turns out, it breaks new ground in potable filth. I get as far as discovering that yes, drain cleaner and marzipan can be found in the form of an alcoholic drink, before reflexively tipping the rest down the sink, an action I almost never perform in the real world. Toxic is the only word.

And then I sit and stare angrily at the still fairly full Crème de Pêche bottle, and at the thirty remaining Tesco Cavas. Who would have thought it could be so challenging?

The Joy of
Wine Browsing

PK

There is a nearby wine merchant posh enough to have an ampersand in its name. The manager has the physique of those nourished without a concern for cash, contained within an inevitable striped shirt. He sweeps out from behind the counter to intercept visitors, with an extraordinary combination of the grovelling of Uriah Heep and the swagger of a Pall Mall club porter ('Are you *entitled* to be here, sir?'). And before one can orientate oneself between the Bordeaux and the bargain bins, he asks: 'Can I help you?'

No. You cannot help me. I am not looking for anything specific; I am browsing. I do not need to be monitored like a potential shoplifter, and I certainly do not wish to be escorted around the shelves to the accompaniment of a running commentary. There may be a purchase somewhere in the offing, but at the moment, thank you very much, I am just looking.

What is the point of 'just looking' at wines that are created in order to drink?

10

Well, first, an education. Have you ever compared the colour of five vintages of Château d'Yquem? Did you know they make half-bottles of Château Lynch-Bages? Have you noticed how the Rothschilds are inspired by the style of the Lafite label on their lesser wines? Or the undiscovered wines which carry in small type the names of winemakers like Moueix and Chapoutier? These are all things I have learnt through browsing.

I have remembered more about the relative prices of wines, regions and vintages by browsing than I ever have from lists. Somehow the visual element of a label, on a bottle, in a store registers those things more clearly in my mind.

Browsing gives you a good indication of the nature of a merchant. The presence of one or two great wines on their shelves establishes benchmarks, of price, good taste, long-standing and industry connections, which enable you to put the rest of their offering into perspective. One of the sure signs of the collapse of Oddbins was the absence of any recognisable wines in their shops.

And then there is an almost emotional element to browsing – imagining the wine, the flavour, the occasion. Simply being in the presence of wines you are trying to understand, may never be able to afford, and sometimes find it hard to believe even exist. Have you actually *seen* a bottle of Screaming Eagle, which is allocated only to those on its waiting list? Or a 1961 claret, one of the greatest vintages of the last century? People thrill to first editions not because they want to read the contents, but because that's how the book first appeared. Surely wine's even better, because every vintage is a first and *only* edition.

There are plenty of things people simply look at, without ever using them for their intended purpose. No one spends their coin collection. People wander around commercial art galleries without the intention (or indeed the wealth) to buy the items on display. Secondhand bookshops depend upon browsing, and people flick happily through the racks in record shops without anyone feeling the need to offer fatuous advice. ('Looking for a record beginning with B then, sir?')

I am not a timewaster; except in the sense that the only person's time I am wasting is my own. I won't waste the staff's time, because I don't need to *occupy* their time. So if you happen to recognise yourself as the chap who runs Pompous & Disdain (Wine Merchants), may I suggest (ever so 'umbly) that the phrase 'Let me know if you need any help . . . ' is much better. I will indeed let you know, and may then actually buy something.

But sometimes it's hard. On a recent trip to Paris I made a pilgrimage to Les Caves d'Augé. Opened in 1850, it's the oldest wine store in Paris, and was Proust's local. I've always loved the French phrase for window-shopping – *lécher les vitrines* or, literally, to lick the windows – and that's about all one can afford to do in Paris these days. But in Augé, it's actually quite hard even to browse. It's two wonderful old, crowded rooms, each piled to the ceiling with dusty bottles, like being in someone's actual cellar. The phrase 'kid in a sweetshop' comes to mind, and any parent knows just how long that kid will take to make up its mind.

But the staff hover expectantly behind you, watching every move as you shuffle between the cases. Even hiding behind the language barrier isn't enough to dispel their attention. No, I am not going to lift that bottle of Ausone 2005 at €1380 and give it a shake. Like saintly relics, it's enough just to look, to revel in the presence. Leave me *alone*!

I began to think it impossible to browse wine in Paris. But then I passed La Maison des Millesimes, in Saint-Germain-des-Prés, offering a truly spectacular collection of Bordeaux. The shop is off-puttingly bling, but my desire to just see such wonderful vintages overcame its *froideur*. However, when I shrugged off the inevitable offer of help in my poor French, the salesman responded in conversational English; it turned out he was a young Lancastrian, who responded to the presence of a genuine wine enthusiast even if I couldn't afford their spectacular wines.

'Look at this!' he said conspiratorially, and pulled open a drawer to reveal a 1947 Sauternes, its wine the colour of honey, its label held on with clingfilm. We stood there for a moment, just looking at it together, grinning. Just looking.

And then I left.

Minimum Pricing
CJ

Straight to the point: Baron Saint Jean is – or was – a *vin de pays* built out of what are conscientiously known on the label as *regional grapes*, incorporating Grenache and Merlot and a couple whose names I couldn't read, plus possibly some more, not specified. *Good with toad in the hole* a cardboard sign above the shelf announced at my nearest branch of German supermarket giants Aldi, which made a refreshing change from all those reflexive nods to game and cheese, but how do we feel about such candour while we're shopping for wine?

Anyway. I wanted to like this drink for all the obvious reasons – screw top, very cheap, red, unpretentious Aldi sales environment, a general ideological predisposition in favour of modern affordable mass-produced everyday wines – but I have to say that I was getting nervous as I tumbled out into the car park in order to drive my loot away. Why? Because I am starting to acquire a degree of nervousness about very cheap booze in this country, and am wondering if, long-term, I have the constitution for rock-bottom wines. And the Baron Saint Jean was a bit of a test. Handled with extreme care, it was just about drinkable.

14

The first gusts from the neck of the bottle practically blinded me, and if you didn't give it time to shake off the cellulose and vinegar fumes while it was sitting in the glass, your mouth would pucker up like a drawstring pouch. Sipped respectfully, it turned into a blackcurranty kind of sluicing narrowly covering the roof of the mouth, followed by a hot gas blast in the back of the throat, an impression of plastic adhesive, ending with a flourish of underarm deodorant spreading down towards the lungs. Not great, but not something you could feel indifferent towards, either.

Why, then, was I drinking it at all? Apart from the usual reasons? Well, the British government keeps deciding that something must be done about binge drinking in this country. And what it has recently decided is that there ought to be some kind of minimum price attached to alcoholic beverages, to deter people *at a certain level in society* from buying too much of the stuff and going out and barfing all over town centres.

A closed world to me, obviously, because I'm too old and pathetic to go out drinking and fighting and barfing *but*: what struck both myself and PK (quite independently) was the fact that when this story broke, a bottle of red wine was displayed on the BBC News as Exhibit A in the government's case for the prosecution, and this bottle purported to cost no more than a wildly irresponsible *£2.09*. Yes, *£2.09* for a full 75cl bottle of some kind of red grape-based adult beverage.

That *was* pretty cheap, it must be said (although the inhabitants of Spain, France, Italy, Greece and so on would find it provocatively oversold, given the likely contents) and yet I've never seen anything quite as bargain-basement on sale in London. Can you only get this stuff in Doncaster? Nuneaton? Sunderland? Cardiff?

So: how far do you have to go to get near this price in the

South-East; and what's the stuff taste like when you've found it?

Clearly a job for me rather than PK but given that I didn't feel much like exerting myself, I cut to the chase and expedited a bottle of red at Aldi, going for £2.99. The price was near enough – that magical £2-and-something price point – and all I had to do was go to Hounslow to get it.

As for question 2? Obviously (see above) it wasn't good. I normally welcome mass-produced tanker wines as opening up a world of accessible non-elitist cheap'n'cheerful wine drinking. But even I couldn't get on with the Baron.

What, then, is this stuff for? This kind of drink is not a drink anyone would *want* to drink. It is a means to an end: just there to get you into a different psychic state. Which poses another question: if the government were to slap a few more pence in duty on the price of a bottle of (say) the Baron, would it really put off a determined, impecunious, undiscerning wine drinker, whether they wanted to consume the Baron with a nice plate of toad in the hole, or neck it in ten minutes flat and go out and break something? Anyone who drinks this grog from choice will not be easily deterred by an extra 30 or 40p on the price.

I thought I'd never say this, but the problem is less to do with the price and more to do with the terrible quality. The harm-fulness of the wine lies in the fact that it's extremely difficult to treat *as* wine, to develop a more-than-utilitarian relationship with it. You might as well drink anti-freeze or cough syrup, for all the enjoyment there is. And the only way to break a causal connection which posits wine as a drug and not much else – and seriously modify people's behaviour with respect to it – is to treat booze like cigarettes and price it completely out of the market.

Is this really anyone's idea of an intended consequence? Even the British government's?

Six-Bottle Discounts

PK

What is that clanking noise? It is the sound of the indulgent wine drinker, rushing to enjoy a supermarket discount off six or more bottles of wine.

You know when supermarkets are running one of these sporadic offers, '25 per cent off any six bottles', because you will be passed in the street by someone bent almost double, arms like a baboon, clanking like Ernie the milkman. Me.

The sound of clanking has a particular resonance in the world of wine. In the days before security constraints, the clanking of bottles was the soundtrack of the airport departure lounge. People were always lugging back multiple bottles of cheap plonk they had bought on their holiday, ignoring suggestions that 'it won't travel' with a determined 'Yes it bloody well *will!*' They would then struggle to stuff into the overhead locker a barrel bag containing half a dozen bottles of wine, all going in different directions like cats in a sack.

Nowadays, the clanking is the sound of multiple purchase, which has to be disguised when you get back from the shops. You can try the CJ tactic, of calling out as he arrives home, 'I got some more olive oil . . . !' But clanking is what we in the drinking game call a bit of a giveaway.

I presume that when it comes to these six-bottle offers the supermarkets are imagining one of two scenarios. Perhaps you will have the wine delivered – but I shall write anon of my problems with wine deliveries, which invariably come when I am either out or in the toilet. Or perhaps you are simply going to add half a dozen bottles of wine to your trolley of weekly shopping? This is really not advisable when my spouse is pushing said trolley. If you think there are arguments over HS2 . . .

So I set off solo to Sainsbury's on a quiet afternoon to benefit from their offer. Now, you can't really stride back up the High Road with a case of six bottles under your arm. It's that bit too heavy, and that bit too big, and a cumbersome shape to carry as well. And you look like a looter.

But if you unload it into shopping bags, it clanks and clonks as you walk home, announcing to everyone that you buy your booze several bottles at a time.

Oh yes, *we* know it's going into the cellar to drink over weeks and months ahead, but it sounds to everyone else as if you consume in such quantity that you just had to buy half a dozen bottles, there and then. If it was for a special occasion, they think, you would have made a special trip – *in your car*. Plus, of course, as the sound is not muffled, you have clearly bought nothing else. No, to them this is obviously just profligate personal consumption, bought impulsively by a pedestrian.

So this time, I thought I would take and employ a very clever carrier, which has little compartments to hold six bottles – separately, and silently. It's made out of recycled bin liners or something, and is as tough as old boots. In fact, it may even *be* recycled old boots. But unfortunately, though perhaps predictably as it was sold by them, it bears the Majestic logo.

Which was doubly embarrassing. First, because I had to stand at a Sainsbury's checkout loading up a Majestic carrier like some kind of turncoat. The looks! Coming in here when the 25 per cent offer's on . . . This whole reusable bag thing is all very well, until you try loading one up in a rival shop.

And then, I had to walk up the High Road, looking like the kind of idiot who would go shopping at a wine warehouse like Majestic *without a car*. It's one thing to be overcome with self-indulgence at a supermarket, and emerge with half a dozen bottles of wine when you only went in for a loaf. We've all done that. Surely.

But to go to a wine warehouse, which has a minimum purchase of six bottles, without a car? What, you visited Majestic absentmindedly, and suddenly felt you'd forgotten something . . . spectacles? . . . credit card? . . . ah, *car*!

Anyway, I finally struggled home on foot from Sainsbury's, lugging my six bottles – *silently*. Since you ask, I got a lovely mature Chianti Classico Riserva from their Fine Wine selection, with 25 per cent off an already reduced price. Even though it sounds like something which footballers are caught doing in hotel rooms, I believe this is called a 'double dip'. As they say, job's a good 'un.

But I had to make the decision to shop as either a clanking compulsive alcoholic, or a silent forgetful idiot. I chose the latter. (Were it true, I would of course have forgotten the whole experience . . .)

Either way, I appeared to the world as a stooped figure with elongated arms, as if I had only made it halfway along the evolutionary scale.

Which, now I come to think of it . . .

Virgin Wines
CJ

I ordered this stuff from Virgin Wines on the back of a special offer that came with a broadband router gadget. It's true. Trying to get your router to work? Have a drink! It's the logical next step.

Naturally enough, this mail-order wine, dispatched to our house in the London suburbs, with good road and rail connections, didn't arrive, even though Virgin emailed me two days after the order to ask how I was enjoying it: 'I trust everything went well with your recent order,' wrote someone called Jay. 'We'd love to hear from you.' So they heard from me that the drink hadn't come, at which point David, the Priority One Senior Advisor, like a US Air Force officer, got back pretty much instantly – 'Unfortunately it would appear your case has gone missing in transit.' I could have told him that from the outset, given that most of our wine goes missing in transit, but anyway.

No sweat, though, as they ordered up a fresh case of Mixed Essentials, followed by an email from Christopher (Priority One Advisor), advising me that 'Rest assured either myself or a member of the delivery team will be tracking this new case for

you to ensure that any issues that arise are swiftly dealt with.'
What do you know, but the stuff turned up the next day, present
and correct, followed by a *phone call* from a guy announcing
himself as Dave, to check that it was actually there. Now that's
service, sort of.

Not only that, but the case contained a nice black envelope
with the legend *Go on, open me, you know you want to* . . .
printed on the front, and within, a voucher for a clothing and,
yes, lifestyle store, plus £25 off a food-delivery company's first
order. A surfeit of good things.

The wines themselves? To be honest, a bit of a blur. Eight
different varieties, half-and-half mainstream white and red,
Malbec, Merlot, Chardonnay, all sorts. I simply don't have
the mental clarity to hold an opinion on them all. Even now, I
have a bottle of Le Clos Gascon on the go – Merlot and Tannat,
apparently, the latter a grape I had never heard of, big in
Uruguay – *and* a Barossa Valley white. I opened *this* one up
without looking to see what it was, took a mouthful, said to
myself, *Hmm, a Sauvignon Blanc? But not as sawtoothed as
usual*, only to discover that it was a Sémillon Sauvignon Blanc.
Which I guess makes sense. And it's a perfectly approachable
drink, as have they all been, especially at the discounted price of
around £5 a bottle. If I'd paid the notional full price of around
£7? Less convincing. But since we know that wine pricing in
the UK is as transient and unpredictable as ironic laughter, then
fair enough.

The only dealings I can recall having, ever, with Virgin, before
now, were when the whole family (years ago) flew Virgin Atlantic
to San Francisco. At one point it was about 3 a.m. London time
on the plane, almost everyone had passed out – when the Virgin
cabin crew, in their smart red uniforms, woke us all up to offer
us a mint'n'choc ice cream. We were too fuddled and exhausted

to say *No* or *For Christ's sake*. We humbly accepted our ices, ate them, and were, in some cretinous way, grateful for having been woken up in the dead of night and required to eat an entirely inappropriate snack. *Well*, we said, *you don't get that on BA. A woman in a red uniform woke me up with a mint'n'choc ice!* Who cares about the rest of it? Who, indeed, can remember?

So thanks, Jay, Dave and Chris. It's been fun. It's been about the people. And, to some extent, it's been about the wine.

Deliveries

PK

This wine delivery business – it's such a *palaver* . . .

Oh, they make it sound easy. Give your address, name the day, pick your time. But it's so much more complicated than that.

At one time, when I worked in an office, I would have my wine delivered there. Its clanking announced its contents to all and sundry across the open-plan, and no doubt other employees thought this was evidence of a profligate lifestyle typical of senior management.

I'm luckier now, as I often work from home. But it's only a marginal improvement to have a delivery van arrive outside one's house, proclaiming its provenance in its paintwork. Every curtain-twitcher in the street can see you're having a load of wine delivered, and can assemble their own little bundle of judgements as to your wealth, lifestyle and alcohol consumption. (Later confirmed, of course, by examination of your recycling box . . .)

However, I can now theoretically name a day and pick a time when I will be home. And, significantly, when Mrs K will be out. So as not to trouble her, unnecessarily, with concerns about infelicitous expenditure, and overindulgent consumption. The wine can then be spirited into the cellar, where its presence will not be detected amongst the bottles which are Not To Be Touched.

I have now had experience of completing several sets of merchants' instructions for wine deliveries. Sometimes they make supposedly helpful suggestions, like 'Is there a shed or garage where we could leave it if you are out?' No, there is not – because if the shed or garage had open access for deliveries, I would not be spending my money on wine, but on replacing all of my stolen tools.

Some also offer a two-and-a-half-hour window during which the delivery should occur. This is all well and good, but at some point during that time I am going to have to visit the lavatory. Dare I? The last time I tried it, no sooner had business commenced than the doorbell rang. I had to yell loudly enough to be heard down on the pavement that 'I'm in the toilet!', an announcement both surprising and unnecessarily informative to several passers-by and next-door's nanny.

This time, I was sent a very nice text, to tell me that my wine would arrive between 12 and 2.30 p.m.

At 11.15, the doorbell rang.

There outside the house is the emblazoned van, informing the neighbours that my consumption is now so great I must have wine delivered a dozen bottles at a time. And there inside the house is Mrs K, still working in her study.

Here's a word of advice for couriers. Wine is like a baby – better delivered when due.

Fortunately, I was not in the toilet. Also fortunately, I was closer to the front door than Mrs K.

Speed was of the essence. 'Anything to sign?' I asked brusquely, anticipating one of those ridiculous handheld electronic devices they ask you to 'sign' with a stylus. (Few of us have experience of writing on glass, apart from the 'yoof' who etch tags on to bus windows, and they are more likely to be recipients of a custodial sentence than a wine delivery.)

'Just this piece of paper. They asked me to have one of those electronic things, and I said, "How'd you expect me to hold that *and* a case of wine?"'

Well, let's not get into that on my doorstep right now, thank you very much. Last month we had 15 metres of skirting board delivered, and that chap managed it, but to be honest I just want to get this case inside and downstairs, before . . .

'Is that something for me?' Mrs K's dulcet tones precede her steps downstairs. I am caught in the hallway, case in hands, like a dog with a string of sausages.

'What?'

'That box.'

I think I would be pushing my luck were I to retort, 'What box?'

'Ah. No. It's just, er, a case of wine actually . . . '

'Oh! A case of wine. A *case*.' This emphasis does not mean that she suffers any category confusion about the actual concept of a case of wine. No: it is to convey that to her, 'case' suggests a suspect level of both consumption and expenditure.

Fortunately, my salvation is staring me in the face – almost literally, since I still have a case of wine clutched to my chest. On the top of the box is a sticker. In most cases, I would be embarrassed by it, since obviously I aspire to be the kind of person whose cases are labelled something like '12 x Latour'. However, this one reads 'Under £6 Reds'.

I gesture towards it with my chin. Mrs K observes, then moves on, with a departing, descending 'Hmmm . . . ', which, roughly translated, means 'All right – *this* time . . . '

SEDIMENT

I take the case downstairs, and stash my embarrassingly cheap bottles away. But I wonder: why not save us all a load of trouble, and put those stickers on *every* case . . . ?

A Tale of
Two Tastings
CJ

One: So here we are, back in the South of France, just under the shoulder of Mont Ventoux, and our chums say, *Let's go to this* cave, *they're advertising Champagne, no, not* méthode Champenoise *but actual Champagne,* so we say, *Fantastic, we haven't been to a* cave *since almost this time last year, with you, as it happens,* and off we go, down a deeply rutted French track, throwing up dust and gravel, sweltering slightly insanely in the heat, before drawing up in front of a nobly proportioned but apparently derelict *château* with an industrial crane sticking out of the top.

But what do you know? This is a work in progress: and yes, as we step over some power cables and a length of hose-pipe, it turns out that the Château la Croix des Pins is indeed in business, and has set out its stall in a freshly painted antechamber, formerly the private *chapelle* of the château – with, as a token of lingering piety, a couple of plaster seraphim on the wall behind the cash register.

What's more, the instant we clear our throats, a very *soignée*

27

young woman bursts out of a side door and starts flogging us the Château la Croix des Pins wine range, plus the champagne they seem to have the concession for down here, *plus* some gluey-looking stuff from Tunisia. She tells us a tale of decline and rebirth: the previous owner of the winery dies, the house starts to fall down, some bright young gunslingers with a hand in other wine-producing regions (hence the heterogeneous mixture) take over, they rebuild and re-invigorate the brand, and their stuff costs €7 and upwards a bottle. Her rhetoric is so seamless and so determined that we lapse into an admiring stupor as she collects more glassware, plus a bucket, plus more wines which we taste, repeatedly extending our glasses for a refill.

Actually, she (correctly) identifies me as the lustreless goob of the party and soon stops my refills, concentrating her energies on our markedly smarter friends. Who, in due course, buy some red and some champagne, and we all go home. And the red (not that it's my place to criticise) tastes fine in what I think of as a light, Grenache-y way, nothing to make you tear your shirt off, but fine.

Two: I wander into my local Majestic Wine Warehouse. I am the only person there (a Monday morning, admittedly, and raining) but I am mercifully left to dicker around with the tasting wines, including a 2000 Chinon, a wine about which I know less than nothing, and which I consume in kingly solitude, noting that it is a) pretty nice and b) too expensive. At no point does anyone attempt to tell me the story of the chilly West London shed which Majestic have made their own. Nor does anyone slyly withhold the glassware from me at the tasting stall. There are no *soignée* young women, just a bloke in fishpaste-coloured shorts. Mildly glowing with Chinon, and glad to have been left alone, I scale down my pretensions and buy some 2009 Domaine Les Yeuses Merlot/Syrah Pays d'Oc.

This reveals itself later in the day to have a nose full of tar and tobacco, a mild cluster-bomb effect on the palate and gums, and a pleasingly cough-mixture finish. In other words, at £7.49 a bottle (including discounts) it is approximately £2 over my Platonic price point, but still worth it.

The problem, insofar as there is a problem, lies back in France, in their interpretation of tasting, the *dégustation et vente* you see all over the wine-growing regions.

How? Well, I used to cling to the idea that *dégustation et vente* allows you to try a wine and meet its producer without the same mercantile pressure that you experience when buying something in a wine shop. Of course, in a *cave*, there's no escape from being eyeballed by the hungry proprietor, but I still like to imagine it as a meeting of individuals, rather than doomed participants in an ineluctable transaction.

And when we rocked up at Château la Croix des Pins, frankly, I was desperate to buy some drink, any drink, if only because it's a cuddly, touristy thing to do and I wanted that kind of transaction, that escape from the Anglo-Saxon condition, that intimacy (however fake) with the wine-maker.

Instead it became one of those typically French encounters in which the proprieties are at least as important as the product itself. One has this feeling of being cleverly manipulated by a high-end salesman – however nice and Frenchified one's hostess is, however much she fans out her fingers and elaborates the magical story of the vineyard – and that *one should appreciate the privilege.*

Which leaves me wondering, what *is* a tasting, a *dégustation*, anyway? Is it a chance to try out new stuff and attempt to talk wine with an expert? Or is that too naive? Wouldn't it make more sense just to assume that the *dégustation* isn't really happening and face up to the fact that it's all about the *vente* and and everything else is a bonus?

The Mixed Case

PK

The festive season had taken its toll upon my wine cellar. I clearly needed to replenish what I like to think of as 'her infinite variety'. But the season had also taken an equivalent toll upon my bank balance. The obvious, simplest thing to do was to buy a mixed case of a dozen cheap bottles. But ay, there's the rub.

Because to me, mixed cases are a suspect entity. They are the libertines of the wine world, offering carefree promiscuity over serious commitment.

We don't purchase mixed selections in many areas of consumption. We commit to a particular variety. We never quite know which sandwiches we'll make during a week, but we don't buy loaves of bread comprising two slices each of white, wholemeal, seeded and rye. We are not offered a bag of mixed meats, six white and six red.

And selections have always troubled me, because they invariably contain some things you don't want. Like Christmas hampers; the providers lay out all of the contents like a wedding photo, and somewhere in the back row you can just spot the things that no one actually wants – the dodgy preserved fruits, the iffy jar of chutney, the tin of pineapple in syrup.

Like boxes of chocolates, hiding their Yardley-flavoured crème centres, which taste as if you've just licked your gran. Or like 'variety' packs of cereals which, to my intense childhood irritation, and carefully hidden on opposite sides of the multipack, always contained two packets of boring corn flakes. Thanks to such instances of selection abuse, I have always had a suspicion of mixed cases of wines.

I know I am a cynic, for whom the light at the end of the tunnel must be seen as a train coming the other way. But wouldn't any merchant take this opportunity to offload his duff wine in a corner of a mixed case? The overpriced non-seller, whose subsequent discount will make a mixed case look more of a bargain? Or the simply shoddy plonk, which a customer might then forgive as one bad bottle out of twelve?

And what the mixed case suggests about the merchant is nothing compared to what it says about the purchaser.

Everything about the mixed case suggests failings. That you are ignorant; you simply don't know enough about wine to assemble a case yourself that suits you and your lifestyle. You feel some kind of middle-class obligation to have wine in the house, and a mixed case is the easiest way of acquiring a small selection. That you can't be bothered to go through a list yourself and select a dozen bottles. Or that you want the scapegoat of a merchant upon whom you can blame any dud bottles which are subsequently mocked by your guests. 'Oh, I didn't *choose* that one, it came in a mixed case . . . '

And then there are people who are drawn by price and ostensible savings rather than contents. (No names, CJ . . .) Indeed, for those who don't give a monkey's about what they are buying as long as it's discounted, there are now 'mystery cases', where you don't actually *know* which wines you're getting, just that they're supposedly a bargain. It's 'a lucky dip you cannot lose', one merchant says, as if you're buying your wine at the fairground.

(The latest I was offered was a case for £79.99, 'with contents worth at least £94.99, and possibly up to £140.99'. I admire the judicious use there of the word 'possibly' . . .)

Anyway, the point of all this is that, in a moment of desperation, to replenish my depleted cellar with modest degrees of both breadth and expenditure, I succumbed to a mixed case.

My excuse was a lack of time in which to assemble a case of my own; my reassurance lay in enjoying the mutuality of The Wine Society, that 'merchant' which exists solely for its members, and so has no reason to palm anything off.

The Society offers a mixed case of six reds and six whites, all under £6, a price threshold so low I'm surprised anything successful apart from a limbo dancer can get under it.

And yet I have found myself drinking eagerly through a variety of consistently interesting and enjoyable wines. I have not encountered a single undrinkable bottle, which, given our success rate at supermarkets for sub-£6 wine, is quite remarkable. Even the inevitable Merlot was drinkable. No great epiphanic discoveries, but no palate-puckering horrors either.

Given their drinkability and their price, they promote these as wines 'to serve without preparation or hesitation', which is absolutely the case, even if hesitation has never offered any previous hindrance to my consumption.

So this is an exercise I may now try again. Far from feeling diminished, my dignity was restored by my temporarily restocked cellar. With the magisterial stride of the cellar master, I could once again proffer a dry white, a rich red or whatever else supper might require.

And all so that, at 8.30 on Sunday evening, I can offer to nip downstairs and bring up something to drink – and Mrs K can turn from the oven and say, 'It's a pity we haven't got a bottle of *cider* to go with this pork . . . '

II

On the
High Street

The High Street
Wine Shop
CJ

I cast my mind back ten years, and I see a thinner, darker-haired, fractionally blither version of myself, limping off to get a bottle of wine, possibly to take to a dinner party, possibly to consume in morbid silence at home. I am spoiled for choice. Within reasonably easy walking distance, there are two supermarkets – a Safeway and a Waitrose – and four free-standing wine shops. There is a Threshers, a Victoria Wine, an Oddbins and a Majestic. There may even be one or two others that I've forgotten. They all sell wine.

Leap forward to the present day, and Threshers and Victoria have both disappeared from our part of town, leaving their premises empty and abandoned, while Safeway, having had a brief fling at being a Morrisons, was rudely turned into an enlarged car park for the even more engorged Waitrose next door. Oddbins at first filled a huge cornershop space, then filled it less convincingly, and finally didn't fill it at all, but handed it over to a wildly over-optimistic independent wine merchant, who did his best to bring the art of fine drinking to our very slightly substandard neighbourhood.

The over-optimistic wine merchant kept it going for a good eighteen months before decamping to the other side of the main road and into smaller, more manageable premises, more befitting his bespoke trade ambitions. Meanwhile, *another* wildly over-optimistic wine merchant succeeded to the ex-Oddbins slot, but with even fewer resources than the first one. Majestic, tucked away from these dissolutions and reformations, picked up the business they lost, and prospered.

But where are we now, right now? Unsurprisingly, the first over-optimistic wine merchant has gone bust. Pizza flyers and double-glazing circulars litter his shop entrance. The second over-optimistic wine merchant is doing his best with a retail space the size of a basketball court and some comfy chairs, but for how long? In the interim, it must be said, not one but two Tesco Metro stores – those little urban stop'n'shops – have taken root. And Waitrose just keeps getting bigger. Thus, we began the decade with four wine stores and two supermarkets. We now have two wine stores, one supermarket, and two chain convenience stores. I am guessing that this is pretty typical of High Street UK.

Is there any reason to fret about this? Patterns of wine consumption have changed out of all recognition in the space of a generation, so why shouldn't the retailing? My parents did their booze shopping in a world of off-licences and one-man suppliers, who kept limited hours and even more limited stock. If you could even find a bottle of Riesling in one of these outlets, the chances were that it was sharing the shelf with a tin of Long Life lager and some Babychams. In the great scheme of things, we haven't lost much. In fact we've gained. So is there any cause for anxiety?

Well, I'm gripped by a feeling that I can't quite rationalise and can't quite shake off: that shopping for wine in a warehouse has stopped being as much fun as it used to be. I can remember going, over a quarter of a century ago, to my first wine warehouse, where I was knocked out by its immensity, its unbelievably exciting range, its stupendous prices, its gritty, authentic, warehouse atmosphere, all concrete floors and industrial lighting. And the fact that you had to buy a minimum of a case, which made me feel like a real grown-up: all that wine and only one liver to deal with it.

Nowadays the warehouses are still there, with the concrete floors and the draughty ambience, but the wines are starting to look a bit familiar, pretty much like the ones you see in the supermarkets, and the prices are okay but not magical, and the draughty ambience is starting to seem less like a justifiable approach to great value retailing and more like a convention, a reflex, another bit of branding rather than the expression of an ethos. You know what I mean. It's not exactly special.

I like wine warehouses. My heart still quickens when I pass one. If they disappeared I would be upset, partly because it would mean losing something I was attached to and partly because the whole retail ecosystem of the country, would dwindle.

Except, except. How sentimental can anyone afford to be? Maybe my kids will come to regard our notion of a high-street wine merchant with as much amused condescension as I grant the memory of the off-licence with my dad bumbling in on a Saturday morning to get his soda syphon refilled. If the wine merchant goes the way of the milliner and the draper, does it matter? Why shouldn't we get everything online or from a supermarket chain? Nostalgia is a disease, so let's embrace whatever the future might bring in as sanguine a frame of mind as we can manage. To which end, I unheedingly take another swig from my Waitrose generic Côtes du Rhône and await developments at the big old warehouse down the road.

Befriending a Wine Merchant

PK

When you have sunk to the bottom, you can only go up. Even Sediment, when agitated or disturbed, will rise. In a bid to remind my palate what wine is all about I decided to find a good, complex bottle of wine that I might actually enjoy. An *interesting* wine.

As an aide-memoire to what decent wine is all about, I've been re-reading the late Simon Hoggart's book *Life's Too Short to Drink Bad Wine*. Well, not on the Sediment blog, it's not, old chum. Not my life, anyway.

In between making me obscenely jealous of the wines he had tasted, Hoggart also offered advice, including the following: 'If you have an independent merchant near you, or a good well-run branch of a chain – the sort that trains its staff and keeps them – make friends.' Now, from my parents to my business partner, people throughout my life have exhorted me to 'make friends', usually with complete failure resulting in a sandpit fight. Or its adult equivalent.

Nor can I say that I am 'friends' with any other shopkeepers. I have been to our local paint shop several times, but I am still treated as a stranger. Mind you, I have never gone in with what I suspect might be a memorable request for 'an interesting paint' . . .

Nevertheless, I thought I would try out Simon Hoggart's principle in order to purchase a wine which, in both senses, was not bad. So I entered my local merchant's, with the lazy gait of the *flâneur* who has nowhere better to be, and an ingratiating grin.

The assistant certainly looked as if he was trained – he had clearly been taught that his job description was best fulfilled behind the counter, and not outside having a smoke. Nor was he glumly perusing his P45. ('Ah no, mate, interesting wine comes in next week – but I'm afraid I'm off to work up the road, in the paint shop . . .') All systems go, then.

I explained that I was looking for something of a treat, something complex I could drink by itself. He asked what kind of thing I liked, and I said I really liked old clarets with a backbone, like Saint-Estèphes. He immediately offered me a 2002 Médoc, which I felt smacked of the obvious rather than the interesting. Then he proposed a Tuscan, a much more stimulating idea.

I said 'Hmm . . . ?' in a quizzical manner, meant to suggest, 'Perhaps you have something even more interesting hidden away for your *friends*?' Clearly this was misinterpreted as 'Can I spend a little more?' It led to the offer of an extremely expensive mature rioja.

It was actually I who suggested a Shiraz/Viognier made by Terlato & Chapoutier. I had seen this mentioned on an American website as one of the best value wines of the year. (Not cheapest, but best value, a distinction lost on certain wine writers.) And I was intrigued by whether comfortable

Australian Shiraz had been lifted into something a bit more complex by a great French winemaker.

'Ah, now that *is* an interesting wine,' he agreed. He went on to say that it was an unoaked Shiraz, which meant you could drink it younger, and that the Viognier added primarily to the nose.

Reasonable guidance – but what made this wine interesting to me was the union between one of the great old winemaking names of the Rhône, and an enthusiast from the New World. Like that duet between Bing Crosby and David Bowie. (Well, that was a bit ropey, actually, but you get my point.) What happens when the traditional skills of France meet the modern, affordable produce of Australia?

He suggested opening it an hour before drinking – and added that 'opening' really meant pouring it into something like a glass, with greater surface area. All of which was extremely good advice.

As he wished me an enjoyable evening, I liked to think that our exchange had gone beyond the merely fiscal. I couldn't say he'd become my *friend* – but perhaps, and who can blame him, he was a little wary of the unctuous grin.

The wine itself was absolutely delicious, and everything I wanted – a reminder of how enjoyable wine can be, and a genuinely interesting treat. And as to my burgeoning friendship with the chap in the wine merchant, I will try to remember to report whether he remembers me if I go back, or ushers me outside to avoid upsetting other customers.

SPAR

CJ

Not for the first time, PK gets one of his mad enthusiasms, insisting that he's found something that I cannot afford to pass up and that, whatever it is, it has got me written all the way through it like a stick of rock. Turns out he's referring to the SPAR Winefest rather than a Bentley, but I am no match for his implacable energies and have to admit that, yes, an hour spent poking around a supermarket chain looking for rock-bottom wines is pretty much my idea of a good time.

The associated SPAR press release waves its arms frantically as it announces 'a host of fantastic quality SPAR brand wines' to be 'backed by extensive marketing support including consumer press advertising, POS material, in-store tastings and PR'. Apparently, 'SPAR's spring Wine Festival earlier this year saw sparkling success', while 'as a mark of their fantastic quality, a host of SPAR brand wines have been recognised by the international wine trade this year'.

SPAR is actually a Dutch company, its name originally DE SPAR, an acronym for *Door Eendrachtig Samenwerken Profiteren Allen Regelmatig*, or 'Everyone Regularly Profits Through United

Collaboration,' which has a nice 1930s collectivist ring to it. You tend to find SPARs in largish villages, smallish towns, the less flashy bits of the bigger cities.

In fact it takes me a while to locate my nearest SPAR, which although not a million miles away as the crow flies, involves a forty-minute drive of scarcely plausible complexity at the end of which I find myself parking my car round the back of an Isthmian League football ground amid a heap of yellowing newspapers and discarded crisp packets. As I walk away from it, I turn and raise my hand in tremulous farewell, expecting never to see the vehicle again.

On the other hand, I am right next door to the SPAR, which turns out to be a local micromart with a few sausage rolls slumbering in a warmer and some copies of *Closer* on the rack. The in-store wine tastings and PR are either not there or so subtly done that they are invisible. In fact, wine of any sort is almost invisible, cunningly spread over three different locations within the store in such a way that it keeps coming as a surprise to me to find anything stronger than Listerine on the shelves.

Still. I elbow aside a pensioner and an obese schoolchild and get down to business. There is a dusty knot of wine giveaways (two for a tenner, white *and* red) on a shelf at about knee height but no, I am strong and head remorselessly for things that look like they might be part of the big SPAR Wine Event. I find the usual suspects – Wolf Blass, Gallo brothers' Turning Leaf, that kind of thing – but no again, you can get these anywhere, especially at the local newsagent, whereas what I want is something authentically SPAR. Eventually, after what seems like a lifetime of fuddled probings under the increasingly scornful gaze of the guy behind the counter, I find a bottle of Valencia Vino Tinto at £5.49 and another of Valencia Vino Blanco for a mere £4.99. Both 'Hand Selected by Wine Experts for SPAR' it says comfortingly on the label, and although the choice in this particular outlet is *nothing like* the range listed on the SPAR website (e.g. the SPAR Bronze Award-winning Chablis, or the SPAR Commended Montepulciano, with full heavy-breathing text accompaniment), it's near enough and the stuff comes home with me.

Taste sensations? Could be worse: the white (no grape varieties named) gives you a spritz of citrus at the start with a quick burp of acidity at the end and nothing much in between, but there's nothing wrong with that. Similarly, the red (no grape varieties named) has a bit of Fruit Gums, a bit of Sarson's Malt Vinegar, and a nice, chesty finish that can be felt between the shoulder blades. It does the job, and what else did I expect? I mean, if Waitrose can make me feel that they're doing me a favour when they sell me their everyday-drinking bargain booze then I'm not going to complain about SPAR's more self-effacing take on the same stuff.

My only grievance is nothing much to do with the wine and more to do with SPAR's half-arsed, indeed, faintly tragic, idea of what constitutes a promotion. Where are the tables with gingham tablecloths? Where are the glossy brochures? I mean, they've got something worth celebrating: a selection of borderline drinkable wines at marginally approachable prices. Let's not hide it like a guilty secret among the Dreft and the Maltesers. Let's get behind it. Let's be proud, in a low-rent kind of way. Let's shout it from the rooftops, or failing that, from the junction of the A238 and the A2043, just south of Norbiton Station.

Marks & Spencer

PK

Like many English boys, I grew up hating Marks & Spencer. Now I'm middle-aged, do I have to succumb to their wine? To say nothing of their elastic-waisted trousers . . .

Marks & Spencer are hailed universally for the quality of their goods; so it's perfectly credible when a respected wine critic suggests that M&S may be currently selling the best value Pinot Noir in the world. It's credible, it's financially appealing (£8.99!), and its only problem is years of ingrained prejudice against M&S. Which, as a middle-aged man and potential core customer, it's perhaps time I overcame.

Kids, you see, often hate M&S. Because when they want some overpriced hip brand of clothing, their parents insist instead on buying them good-quality, cheaper versions from M&S – which *almost* look the same. This makes the children a playground laughing stock. See a teenager wearing M&S jeans, see a victim of bullying in waiting.

But then, as you grow older, and start working and earning, Marks & Spencer pulls you in from a different direction. For the aspirational young professional is lured into M&S not by their clothes, but by their food.

It may be worth taking a moment to try to explain Marks & Spencer food to readers from our former colonies and elsewhere. Unlike their largely practical clothing, M&S food is unashamedly indulgent. They are known mainly for their ready-made dishes, which as their TV ads once breathily intoned, is not just food – it is *M&S* food. This means it is very good, but also very expensive. To illustrate the cash-rich, time-poor nature of customers of their pre-prepared food, one need only look at the frightening price of, say, their pre-roasted potatoes – at the time of writing, £4.98.

And their notion of 'pre-prepared' can be as broad as, say, peel, chop and put in bag. Hence, and I kid you not, their bags of pre-cut carrot batons . . .

The thing is, M&S food is really food for yourselves. Most people would feel 'cheated' if they went out to dinner and someone served them pre-prepared M&S food. It looks as if you have made no effort. Well, you *have* made no effort. Unless you count queuing.

What, then, about a recognisably M&S wine? The store consistently wins awards for its wines – but again, the 'no effort' issue rears its head. Rightly or wrongly, it looks like an afterthought. Turn up at a dinner party bearing a bottle of Marks & Spencer wine, and it looks like you popped in to get some elasticated – sorry, Active Waist – trousers, and grabbed a bottle of wine just because you were there. No effort. Social *faux pas*.

So why, I ask myself, why do they always declare on the label that it *is* an M&S wine? Some kind of misguided brand status? 'We take the awards, you take the praise,' they announced in one of their wine ads. Praise for what? Your ability to find an M&S? Your disposable income? Your understanding of the command, 'Cashier number *four*, please'?

CJ once declared his taste for an M&S House Red; but in his house, spying an M&S bottle is something of a relief, given the menagerie that usually parades across his labels, announcing another ugly compromise between flavour and finance.

At least in one's own home, one can decant a wine and hide its label. If this really is 'the best value Pinot Noir in the world', then I will happily disguise its provenance. If it *looks* like it could be Burgundy . . .

Few people go to M&S specifically to buy a bottle of wine. I can honestly say that I was the only person in my (lengthy) queue holding *just* a bottle of wine. Most people are clearly buying their supper, an entire meal for one or possibly two; I looked embarrassingly as if my whole evening was going to be spent with only a bottle of wine.

(I must just relate the story of the chap arriving at a checkout with a basket containing a small loaf of bread, a half-bottle of wine and a pre-prepared meal for one. 'Single, are you?' asked the checkout girl.

'Yeah,' said the chap, 'Can you tell from the food?'

'No,' she replied. 'You're just bloody ugly.')

Anyway, it has to be said that the Palataia from M&S *is* a delicious, fragrant Pinot Noir. It has a light, strawberry bouquet with a hint of spice, all elements which carry through to its delicate, easy, almost ethereal flavour. It is as good as many Burgundies. It received fulsome praise from Mrs K, who then drank too much of it. No, it is not Labouré-Roi Échezeaux Grand Cru 2007, which I pretentiously told CJ tasted like choral evensong; but it is, as they say, singing from the same hymn sheet. And, even though a single bottle was actually £9.45, that is one-tenth of the Burgundy's price. Very good value indeed.

But. It does not like being decanted for long. That fragrant delicacy disappears like smoke after an aerated hour. You really should serve this to a gathering, and from the bottle. Which means revealing where you got it.

And I can't do it yet. I just can't. Any more than I would pour it wearing shoes which *almost* look like Sperry Top-siders. Giving up the effort, like succumbing to Active Waist trousers, means abandoning the reward.

So – recommended for those who would serve, in M&S terms, not just pork, but a prime cut of Scottish outdoor-bred pork matured for tenderness, de-boned and tied to make carving easier. For family, therefore, not guests.

For guests, you'd surely want to go the whole hog.

Nicolas

CJ

There's no getting away from the grip of nostalgia. In fact I am returning its grisly squeeze this time by staggering about a mile up the hill to our local branch of Nicolas Wines to see what they've got on offer. Why? Because I have been seized by a horrible ungovernable yearning: Nicolas was the first wine I can remember consuming at home, with my parents, in a domestic context – the first wine that, so far as I was concerned, ever made it through the front door of our house – and I want a trip down memory lane. Why now? I have no idea.

The significance of Nicolas decades ago was less to do with the taste (I must have been about seven when it first appeared, so had to drink it adulterated with tap water, and it couldn't have tasted worse if it had been adulterated with Gloy Gum – slightly less terrible in fact, as Gloy wasn't bad if what you wanted was a quick adhesive rush) and more to do with the change it provoked in the atmosphere around the table. At the time, Nicolas spent big on advertising that showed a little three-wheeler delivery van plying the streets of Paris, bringing Nicolas to every address, much as the Unigate Dairy brought two pints of milk to suburban London; only this was a couple of litres of bright, serviceable wine, and Nicolas was its name, and it was, if you believed the copy, the wine the whole of France thrived on.

So my father bought some, and it came in these shapely yet modestly adorned bottles with foil seals (like the foil on the tops of the innocent milk bottles) and little plastic stubs for stoppers. The first one was opened and placed carefully on the sideboard, like a loaded cannon, while we ate our Sunday roast. The effect was immediate. Up to that point, my father had tended to drink beer with his lunch (beer from a freaking great brown bottle with a screw-shaped rubber bung, I might add) while my mother inhaled a gin and tonic. Now, though, we had an emissary from the great wine-making continent of Europe in the room and suddenly, by association, we were at once more sophisticated than we had ever been before, even allowing for the presence of my mother's sprouts. After that, we never looked back. We started taking our holidays abroad and my father grew some rather defensive sideburns. We became worldly.

So this is the legacy of Nicolas. Decades have passed since those interminable Sunday lunches and Nicolas, which started out in Paris in 1822, has itself been through a few changes – especially in this country, where the Nicolas chain of shops recently acquired a new, UK-based owner. The original link with France has thus been formally broken, although the shops still bear (for now, at least) the branding and the claret-y paintwork of the last century, and seem much like any other pleasant, fast-disappearing, off-licence.

What they don't have, and haven't had for ages, are Nicolas-branded wines, least of all in the big, artisanal bottles of child-hood memory. Instead, they have a bargain line called *Les Petites Récoltes*, which cuts, effectively, the crap, offering everyday drinking at a just-about semi-sensible price.

Well. I bought a bottle of their *vin de pays* de la Cité de Carcassonne and took it home and opened it and drank a bit and in no sense was it offering any competition to your user-friendly New World cornershop wines, being instead furious with acidity and alcohol and also a (not unpleasant) taste of burning leaves. I wrote down the words *almost depraved* at one stage, before corking the stuff up and having a lie-down.

But I had to come back to it. I don't know why, but there was something perversely charming about this stuff. It didn't taste like anything commonplace or even expected (turns out it contained every grape known to man: Carignan, Grenache, Cinsault, Cabernet Sauvignon, Merlot), it made no compromises at all, but what it did do, magically, was suggest some kind of barbarous old-school *vin de table*, the sort mythically offered at out-of-the-way rural eateries that everyone except me has managed to find somewhere in France, where the menu is what the *patron* decides to stick on a plate in front of you and where the drink is unlabelled and unknowable and borderline undrinkable, and yet satisfying somehow, and actually quite potable when taken with some (nice, greasy) food, the whole combining into a complete gustatory experience.

Cunning marketing had much to do with this in the case of *Les Petites Récoltes*. The bottles were made of no-frills clear glass, there was almost no labelling, and what labelling there was, was confined to two tiny scraps of coloured paper covered in twirly French handwriting – a rusticity which I'm sure was dreamed up in an office in La Défense, but which does the job for me, almost too potently. Not only did I put up with the bottle's persistently dribbly neck, I welcomed it as a confirmation of its rough'n'ready unpretentiousness, just as I welcomed its rough'n'ready contents.

And, just like the old Nicolas, it was selling me a dream of France in the comfort of my suburban home. Was I such a mug to fall for it?

Tesco Express
PK

It may be hard for some of you to accept, but CJ and I are normal people. That's why we spend much of our time on *Sediment* consuming and considering wines which are neither excessively expensive, nor excessively rare – and, consequently, not excessively good.

And like other normal wine drinkers, we do not necessarily have the wines we would like at hand. The wines in my own (tiny, Mrs K, tiny) cellar are not for drinking. Yet. They are all either too young, too expensive or, I hope, too good to accompany a normal midweek supper, comprising the remains of Sunday's gammon, with egg and chips.

Despite its similarity in price to pizza, no one seems prepared to whiz round to us on a moped with a single bottle of wine. (Now *there's* a business opportunity . . .) And hence, I need to go out and buy a bottle, like a normal person – the kind of normal person, that is, who uses words like 'hence'.

So I am thrown upon the resources of a high street that seems to be able to provide, at eight in the evening, a tub of ice cream of consistently good quality at a competitive price – but not an equivalent bottle of wine.

My local Tesco is called a Tesco Express, a nicety that may be lost on some readers. 'Express' is used to differentiate my little Tesco from a Tesco Extra, Metro, Super, Pennypincher or whatever other suffix they come up with. It is not, in fact, faster; it is simply *smaller* than some of the others in their hierarchy, and therefore lacking any of the promoted or reviewed wines they might have in a Tesco Massive.

So I am faced with the usual sad choice of the branded and the blended. But then I notice a kneeling assistant, assiduously putting bright yellow stickers on to a bottle which I can consequently only see is called 'Sicil . . . Vino Rosso Si . . . '

I thought for a moment she might be applying a recently won *Decanter* award, or, at the very least, a price reduction. But no; this was a sticker proclaiming that the bottle is 'Security Protected'.

Now, I have been fooled before by a supermarket's security protection on a bottle of wine, when I naively thought it might suggest a classier, more valuable product. But this bottle costs £4.15.

Why would anyone, faced with a display of wines, some as eye-wateringly expensive as £10.99, steal the one that costs just £4.15? I asked the girl putting on the stickers, who simply replied, 'Believe me, they'll nick anything.'

Well. What a heartwarming view of one's clientele. Presumably this embodies one of Tesco's stated corporate values, to 'understand customers'.

My local shoplifters clearly need a little enlightenment themselves, in the effort/reward ratio. Surely one bottle is as easy to steal as another; why steal one of the cheapest?

Or could it be that the eyes of the impecunious are instinctively drawn to the cheaper items on a shelf; then, when they realise they can't afford even that, they steal it – without ever having looked at the more expensive stuff?

Anyway, the effect was to make me feel that I was in the kind of place where people would steal a £4.15 bottle of wine. Which must be a pretty lowly place. Remind me next time to bring both my Tesco Clubcard and my stab vest.

I paid for my bottle, like a *normal* person, intrigued as to what 'Sicil . . . Vino Rosso Si . . . ' might taste like. It was, as I had begun excitedly to deduce, a Sicilian red wine. And it was incredibly . . . bland. A light cherry bouquet, and then a soft, barely detectable, blackcurranty flavour. None of that cheap vino alcoholic clench; more like sugar-free Ribena. The label says it 'shows' flavours of red fruits; I prefer the verb 'suggests'.

This is the most drinkable, if least memorable, of all the sub-£5 wines it has been my sorry misfortune to drink. In most instances its consumption would be a pointless exercise, save in the pursuit of inebriation. But in terms of accompanying my supper, it succeeded in the same manner as, indeed, a successful shoplifter – by lacking any noticeable presence.

Was it worth it? Not, was the tasteless wine worth £4.15 a bottle; that's an almost academic question. But I'm left wondering whether it is worth a normal person being regarded as a potential thief amongst thieves in order to buy it.

However, I should just say that Mrs K claims no normal person would drink a glass of wine with gammon, egg and chips. She says a normal person would have had a cup of tea.

Lidl

CJ

Another day, and the old itch returns and nothing will stop it but I must find some really bargain grog and drink it and somehow take pleasure in it as a way of asserting my belief in the existence of a benign but basically cheapskate universe. So. Where to look? I have been disappointed with Aldi in the past, but have had good times with Carrefour, SuperU and, of course, Lidl. Carrefour and SuperU not being in England, I must therefore Lidl it, but it turns out my nearest Lidl is practically in the West Country. But no matter, because I am so slack-jawed with boredom that any excuse to drive into the outer-outer suburbs looking for something I don't need and very probably shouldn't want, is like a gift from Heaven.

Also it's a chance to re-acquaint myself with the mysteries of Lidl itself. If you can't go abroad, go to Lidl: it's not England, and it's only barely a supermarket as we understand it. The dream-like sensation of seeing familiar things subtly and disturbingly modified never fails. I mean, whoever heard of Crusti Croc Salt Your Own Crisps at Waitrose? Or W5 dishwasher tablets? Or Melangerie coffee? Or Dulano salami? Or Master Crumble

57

breakfast cereal? To say nothing of the possibility of acquiring a Circular Saw with Laser Guide (£34.99) or a tube of Construction Adhesive (£1.99) or a Toilet Seat with LED Lights (£26.99). But Lidl contains all of these things in its parallel universe, and all these things define it. And this is without even touching on the provisional, even guerrilla character of the stores themselves, which look like car-exhaust replacement centres that have gone bust and been converted overnight into food cash'n'carries, filled with the contents of three Czech pantechnicons and lit by the emergency lighting system nicked from a nearby hospital.

But on the other hand: you can (as anyone familiar with Lidl will attest) get some really edible stuff there, for not much. Picking over the roughly opened cardboard crates and cheap trestles, you can find a single malt Scotch Whisky that costs less than a couple of bottles of Waitrose Sauvignon Blanc, and a milk chocolate Fruit'n'Nut substitute that rarely leaves our favourites list. It is like finding gold at the bottom of a bin liner.

And the wines? A small but pertinent choice at my closest Lidl – a good thing, no attempt to bludgeon you to death. Instead there is a score of red, white and pink plus some sparkling stuff, in the middle of which I lunge at a German Pinot Blanc (in a transgressive, weirdly shaped brown bottle, erotic in its perversity) for £4.99; an Australian Shiraz/Cabernet Sauvignon at £3.99; and something calling itself Bordeaux – red, AC, £3.99. These are magic numbers – added to which the £3.99 Bordeaux has instructions *in German* on the back, which makes it as fabulous as something out of Maeterlinck: *Dieser harmonische Rotwein stammt aus einer der berühmtesten Wein-Regionen der Welt.* I am hopeful. I am on a first date.

Perhaps too hopeful. Loads of tannins and acidity, chesty cough/hint of groin strain, notes of old newspaper, dust, socks, are the main impressions. A fifteen-minute pause allows it to fight amongst itself and after that, well, it's about okay. It's a wine that you avert your gaze from while drinking, but it's still recognisably wine. I blame my disappointment on the tragic magic of Lidl, of course, the thing that got me out of the house in the first place, the dream of finding a better, cheaper, bar of chocolate; a toilet seat with LED lights; a bottle of wine costing £3.99 that tastes like a bottle of wine costing £5.49. *Oh reiner Widerspruch, Lust,* as Rilke put it, capturing that Lidl psychic dislocation in one.

Sainsbury's Basic

PK

How attractive any wine looks, in my Café de Flore carafe. It is as if I am about to enjoy a drink at the legendary café on the Boulevard Saint-Germain. Where Sartre and Camus lingered, and where the smallest, cheapest goblet of Brouilly costs €7.50.

If only. My location is actually not Saint-Germain. The contents of the carafe are actually Spanish. The entire bottle actually cost £2.68. This is Basics red wine, from Sainsbury's. Like most supermarkets, this is the range where they claim to provide goods of acceptable quality for the lowest price. And the latter part of that claim is pretty unassailable. At £2.68 a bottle, this is the cheapest wine I have ever knowingly drunk.

But what is 'basic' wine? And why am I disguising it in a carafe from the Café de Flore? We are about to find out . . .

Basics products ('cutting costs, not corners') carry jaunty little explanations of their 'basic' nature. Lemons, for instance, are 'no lookers, great juicers'. In this case, it is 'wine for the kitchen, not the cellar'. Note 'kitchen' − not 'dining room', 'lounge' or even, for the residentially challenged, 'supper table'. Must a wine provoke a whole, socially confusing route around the potential layout of our accommodation?

Or perhaps the idea of keeping it in the kitchen, or disguising its appearance elsewhere in the house, is an acknowledgment of the hideousness of the label, the colour and graphics of which would not happily co-exist with any table setting outside of a cartoon.

There is always a line of cynical thinking, and I am always drawn to it. The line of cynical thinking says that the lurid packaging of value ranges, whether Morrison's, Tesco or Sainsbury's, is actually designed so that people feel embarrassed checking out an entire basketful. It's a loud declaration of poverty to everyone else in the supermarket queue – so that even people who really want to buy a week's worth of Basics feel embarrassed to do so.

Supermarkets can therefore offer cheap products, improving both their image and their relative price rankings, while knowing full well that people will top their basket up with more expensive items.

So in the 'dining room', if you have one, this label would immediately launch a whole set of assumptions which might prejudice an evening's conviviality, from the likely quality of the wine to the parsimoniousness of the host and the dubiousness of any accompanying food. You don't catch many glimpses of the Basics label on *Come Dine With Me*.

So, for all those reasons, I decanted the wine into my lovely Café de Flore carafe. This would allow the wine to breathe, hopefully improving its flavour. It would avoid ribald comments from the rest of the household. And it might help me to forget the provenance of the wine and approach it with an open mind.

Basic wine comes, it seems, from Spain – hence *vino de mesa*. Not wine from romantic-sounding areas with tabletop mountains like Algar de Mesa; no, here *mesa* really does mean 'table', as in table wine. Still, at least we have moved from the kitchen to the table . . .

Sainsbury's themselves describe it as being 'an easy-drinking table wine with light red-fruit flavours'. Now, CJ and I seem to be alone in bringing into the vocabulary of wine description terms such as 'challenging', 'sweaty' and 'fight-inducing'. Nevertheless, I always find this 'easy-drinking' notion intriguing – *what else should wine be?* Few cheap wines honestly describe themselves as 'difficult to swallow'.

In the glass, this has an aroma I can only describe as burnt rubber, with its familiar catch in the nostrils, and suggestion of impending disaster. But it has virtually no flavour whatsoever, beyond a vague taste of fruit-gums, possibly, but not necessarily, the red ones. As it opens up, a fragrance emerges which is reminiscent of alcohol and wet carpet, like the aftermath of a student party; but still no flavour, until the tang of alcohol finally forces its way through and begins to provoke a mild nausea. And a fast-impending headache.

I now understand both of the notions that eluded me. 'Easy-drinking' means it is like swallowing saliva – a reflex action, virtually unnoticed, and certainly not troubling your palate. 'Basic' means it conforms to the most fundamental definition of wine that Lord Sainsbury can find, *viz*, it is red, it is liquid and it is alcoholic.

III

Containment Policy

In Praise of
the Half-Bottle

PK

Driven perhaps by recent over-indulgence, perhaps by recent austerity, I feel that the half-bottle of wine deserves a reappraisal. Quite apart from constraining my consumption, there are some valid points to be made in celebration of the half-bottle, even if they do bring me into direct conflict with CJ, who seems to prefer the jerry can as a measure.

The thing is, the half-bottle is really a solitary pleasure. There simply isn't enough to share. I have watched disbelievingly as a Parisian couple shared a half-bottle of wine over lunch. (At the other end of this scale, I once nodded admiringly at two City chaps sitting down at Rules restaurant to a serious lunch of steak and kidney pudding and a magnum of claret. Respect.)

Does that mean there's something of the sad and lonely about the half-bottle? Something of the book beside the dining plate, the microwaved meal for one, and the failure to subscribe to BT Friends & Family because you can't make up the numbers?

No; look at it the other way. There's nothing greedy about a half-bottle to yourself. You can sit alone at a table with a half-bottle in front of you, and project an image of totality; neither profligate nor parsimonious, this is my all.

And knowing that it's your all, you can pace your drinking accordingly. We all do it; that's the slug for before, top it up for the starter, leave that for the main . . . you pace yourself according to the quantity of wine at hand. (And hence there is nothing more irritating than a companion who suddenly says, halfway down a bottle, 'Do you know, I *will* have a glass after all?' Oh, so there *won't* be enough left to go with my cheese, then. Suddenly, like a sat nav taken on a diversion, you have to recalculate everything.)

The half-bottle is all yours, to open and complete. Yes, one *could* always decant half of a 75cl bottle, and seal the rest for another day; that still provides you with that satisfying sense of completion, watching the level go down and pacing your consumption until the last drops are wrung from your carafe. But there is something about having an actual bottle on the table, connecting the taste and the label, which a decanter can never provide.

And is it just me (and I often discover it is . . .) but don't you always find that the first 'half' you decant is invariably larger than the second? Is it the difficulty of accounting properly for the quantity in the narrower neck? Or just the excitement of opening a new bottle? Whatever; the half on Day Two is never quite the size of the half on Day One.

The real problem – and let's face it, there always seems to be a problem where *Sediment* is concerned – is that it's hard to get decent red wine in half-bottles. It's too much trouble for a lot of producers to change their bottling lines. The really good stuff needs the size of a bottle (or even a magnum) to mature properly over the years; the bulk wine merchants don't bother stocking half-bottles; and in the supermarkets half-bottles are often just 'cooking wines'.

However, I did discover a wine merchant in the City, whose main role seemed to be providing frighteningly expensive wines for banker types with huge amounts of money. I was in here once (browsing, just browsing . . .) when a chap walked in; the assistant said, 'Good afternoon, sir. Got anything in mind?' and the customer actually replied, 'Oh, about a thousand pounds a case . . . ?'

Anyway, they *did* offer a good selection of half-bottles. Perhaps instead of a moderately good magnum, City boys now limit themselves to a good half-bottle at lunchtime – or perhaps it's to offer something to penniless plebs like me – but there were half a dozen interesting halves of red in the shop, including some serious Clarets – Pichon-Longueville Lalande 2005 at £40.80 a half-bottle, anyone? Apart from that one, the rest were below £20, and there's something exciting to me about seeing a wine list with good Bordeaux priced affordably in the 'teens, even if you are only getting half the quantity.

And perhaps that's the thing; half-bottles are an opportunity to experience wines you couldn't afford by the bottle. Lesser quantity, higher quality; isn't that the New Year resolution of many? Not CJ, I suspect, but if so, perhaps this is the answer. Sometimes, it can be better to do things by halves.

Wine in a Box I
CJ

It's the holidays, and we make our way to France to stay with our pals in the Ventoux region. Here we discover to our horror that their house in the hills is even more eye-wateringly beautiful than the last time we were there, in fact is so glamorous that we wonder if we shouldn't sleep in the car rather than attempt to live up to the bedding in the spare room.

Still. After a day or so we have recovered enough from the shock to be able to loll around the pool and spend a couple of hours over lunch and drink our *apéritifs* on the upper terrace and generally kid ourselves that it wouldn't have taken *that* much effort on our part to achieve the same sun-drenched perfection, we just had different priorities. Then, to add to my bliss, if that were possible, our host says that if I want to buy a quantity of local grog, he'll take it back to England for me in his luxury shooting brake.

Giggling with anticipation, I head straight down to the nearest *cave*, spending only an hour wandering around the adorable tourist honeypot townlet in which it is situated before actually going in to choose the drink. Which means that I am so surfeited with well-being by the time I enter the *cave*, I'm not really in a position to deal with the profusion of wines which suddenly fills my vision.

All I want is a medium *BiB* (as in *Bag-in-Box* as the French call them, i.e. a no-nonsense working man's wine box) of red, another of rosé and a third of white. But (a) I am initially thrown by the luscious high-end Ventoux bottles parked at the entrance and (b) I am subsequently thrown by the presence of two elfin and hypnotically French young women, wrestling with a pallet of *BiBs* in exactly that dingy corner where the cheap grog lives. As a consequence, I gather up two whites and a red instead of a red, white and pink, stagger over to the checkout and only discover what I've done ten days later when our (now former) host drops them off.

My bad, as they say, but since the stuff works out at slightly less than €3 a litre, I can't really complain. But what exactly *is* it? One five-litre container owns up to nothing more specific than *White Ventoux*, plus instructions for getting at the tap. The red, similarly, is just *AOC Ventoux Rouge*. Only the other white, the one bought in error, fesses up to anything: *Viognier Chardonnay*. This is the one that I cram into the fridge, having sawn the top off the box to get it to fit. The red I place on top of the wine rack, no more than half a metre from my elbow while I eat.

I now have more cheap drink at my immediate disposal than I have ever had in my life. I could drink myself stupid every night if I wanted to. Things could not be much better.

Except that, like the stooge in a morality tale, I find myself increasingly beleaguered by the superabundance of my own supplies. The red is pretty much as I hoped for, with that lightness and hint of austerity I associate with Ventoux; the white, on the other hand, gives me mild tinnitus plus a sense of existential doom. Why? It should be fine. I force myself to drink more, in order to desensitise my tastebuds. Over time it seems to become less industrial, perhaps as it degrades in its *BiB* (four weeks is the maximum time you've got, according to the box). But it is a grim, attritional business.

But then (God help us) this raises another, bigger question: *how much am I drinking?* I pour a generous splash into my glass, consume it, pour another, consume it, pour another; I mean there are five litres in there, or there were, and the cardboard is opaque, so in some ways it's a bottomless vat of wine, but in another way it's a nightmare, in which I entirely lose count of how many glasses I've poured myself, and only know that at the end of the evening I feel eighty years old and as if my mouth has been used as a photographer's developing tray.

After several days of this, I work out that what I need is a *pichet*, into which I can pour a metered quantity of drink. A little glass jug catches my eye. I shall find out how much it holds, then determine how much 40cl of wine looks like when poured into it, then use that as my guide. That way, I shall not only retain a measure of self-control at supper time, I shall make my booze last longer.

I take the jug down from the shelf. It looks a bit dusty. There is a small crack next to the handle. My wife, who happens to be passing, says, 'You know we use that to put flowers in, don't you?'

'Yes,' I say, a pathetic note in my voice. 'But I have my dignity to think of.'

And indeed, that evening I sit there full of bourgeois self-importance with my little jug of wine, and everything works according to plan, even though the wine is not only light and austere, but oddly nuanced with a flavour of dust. Only another week to go, I reckon.

Wine in a Box II

PK

In the past, I've been scathing about wine in boxes. Wine in a box? Is that like cigars in a bottle?

So it's ironic that, just a week after CJ returned from France with three wines in boxes, I found myself buying one from Sainsbury's. In a special offer, a box of Caja Roja had been reduced by Sainsbury's from £16 to £12. That's 2.25 litres, or three bottles' worth, for £12. It's the cheapest drinkable wine I have encountered in the UK. It's not the rather superior *Carta* Roja – but it's £4 a bottle. An irresistible bargain. Only it's in a box.

Now on the whole, I have resisted wine in a box. It is, as they say, convenient. It is also, as they say, uncouth. And I do so wish to be couth.

Like many purchasers, I argued to myself that a wine box would be a convenient way of drinking the odd glass, and cooking with the odd squirt, while keeping the rest fresh. The key word here being, again, 'convenient'.

Just a splash of wine in these lentils? Here it is, with its own 'convenient' tap, just as if red wine has been plumbed into the kitchen. A little glass of something with supper? Here again. Pour just as much as you like, and the box will stay fresh. It's so 'convenient'.

But is convenience necessarily a good thing? Velcro is more convenient than buttons, but you don't see much of it on Savile Row.

Wine boxes are not designed for the dining table. They may well offer 'convenience', but you wouldn't serve convenience *food* to your guests.

You also have to hoist wine boxes above glass height, always an ungainly manoeuvre. It's reminiscent of lifting dumbbells, something else not recommended over a laden dining table.

Unlike a magnum of wine, which everyone assumes you are sharing with friends, a box is something people assume you are drinking in privacy. A box is like announcing personal profligate consumption, the equivalent of the giant airport bar of Toblerone.

Yes, you can use your extensive collection of decanters, carafes and *pichets* to disguise your embarrassing secret. But that's not 'convenient', is it? Soon you find yourself tiptoeing back into the kitchen between courses or during ad breaks, directly refilling glass after glass. With no visible record of your consumption.

How long before you're just passing through the kitchen, work to do, clock ticking, stressed out like a cat passing Crufts. Can you be bothered to make a mid-morning coffee? Here, over here, calls the little box on the worktop. Who's to know? And hey, if we're talking convenience, why bother dirtying a glass? We've all drunk *water* directly from a tap . . .

It's a downward path. In its worst case, I recall drinking with someone who, when the flow began to falter, pulled the box apart and, determined to get every last drop, actually wrung out the foil bag inside.

And in the end, the box goes into the recycling, where it is far more troublesome than a straightforward glass bottle, because who's prepared to break it down into its constituent elements of cardboard, foil and plastic? It sits there whole, like a squat badge of shame, announcing to the neighbours your consumption, your poverty and your convenience-driven laziness.

A single bottle of cheap wine might be considered desperation. An entire box of it suggests destitution.

And ask yourself this. If boxes are so good, how come it's only cheap wines that are in them?

So, swings and roundabouts. On the swings, it's astonishingly cheap, perfectly drinkable, and with the added 'convenience' of staying fresh. On the roundabouts, it's clumsy, ugly and suggests something dubious about your drinking.

Me? I'm on the climbing frame.

Plastic Goblets

PK

I suppose all of us must sometimes feel, despite our desire for a glass of wine, that it's just too much hard work to open a bottle, and pour its contents into a glass. Oh, the *effort*. Or perhaps all of one's wine glasses are dirty? Or broken? Or you've forgotten which way round a corkscrew turns? That must be when we reach with a sigh of relief for a serving of wine conveniently prepackaged in a sealed plastic goblet.

This concept once appeared on *Dragon's Den*, a TV programme in which, for the uninitiated, business concepts are 'pitched' to a panel of potential investors. The entrepreneur Duncan Bannatyne said at the time: 'This doesn't work as a selling item. People do not want to buy wine in plastic glasses like that. For that reason, I'm out.'

But of course, he has been proved wrong. I could have told him that, depressingly, there are people out there who will buy wine in *anything*, from cardboard boxes to metal cans, from absurdly shaped and coloured bottles and faux carafes to CJ's jerrycan. A plastic goblet seems positively civilised by comparison.

And despite the Dragons' misgivings, this concept seems to

be proving extremely successful with, the manufacturers claim, 'picnickers, concertgoers and commuters'. I will take their word for the latter, as I haven't myself seen anyone drinking wine on the 237 bus.

But it would seem to me, despite my opening remarks, that the market for sealed plastic goblets of wine is surely an outdoor one. Which was why I was surprised to see it on the supermarket shelves during a bitterly cold December.

Yet Lord Sainsbury, in his infinite winter wisdom, piles these goblets high and sells 'em, if not cheap, then at £2.49 apiece. And upon his informative little shelf-talker, he recommends that they are 'perfect with grilled steak or tomato-based pasta dishes'.

Now, those are not really outdoor dishes, are they, whether in chilly December or not. So they are clearly suggesting that one enjoys this product indoors, with one's warming winter meals. So be it.

I can tell you from the outset, though, that having a plastic glass, with a label on its side, at your table for Sunday lunch, makes you feel a total prannock. (One of the offspring raises the glass, quizzically; Mrs K offers those emollient words, 'It's for the blog,' and they both sit back to watch with barely disguised amusement.)

Obviously you could try to emulate in your home the outdoor situations for which the goblet was presumably devised. You could perhaps picnic in the dining room, by sitting on the floor in an uncomfortable position, pairing your plastic glass with plastic cutlery, and forgetting several vital components of the meal.

You could emulate train commuters, by lurching about in your seat, overcrowding your dining area with newspapers, and having your companion push past you mid-meal to visit the lavatory.

Or you could resist going to the toilet at all, and turn on somebody else's choice of music at inappropriate volume, while, every so often, your companion jumps on your foot. That's the outdoor concert. Or is it the commuting . . . ?

Anyway, the goblet initially is a little challenging. Opening it is rather like opening a pot of yoghurt, or a plastic flagon of milk. Like the milk, the problem comes with removing the very last bit of the foil lid, which jerks free and invariably causes the contents to slop out. Like the yoghurt, one wonders whether it is socially acceptable to lick the lid.

I would like to describe the wine's bouquet, but I can't, because the glass is almost full, and so it is impossible to get your nose inside the glass without getting wine in your nostrils. Loath to share the fate of the Duke of Clarence, who was drowned in a butt of Malmsey, we shall have to forgo notes on the bouquet.

And the goblet is also somewhat uncomfortable in the mouth. In order for the lid to adhere, the rim of the goblet is flat, not rounded – again, like a yoghurt pot – which means that it catches on your upper lip as you drink. It is akin to drinking from a plastic flowerpot.

But astonishingly, the wine itself is actually drinkable. It's a pretty straightforward Shiraz – a bit light in weight, but with distinctive fruit and spice, and no evil catch in the throat. The plastic seems to have had no more discernible impact on the flavour than on beer in a plastic glass, or water from a plastic bottle. Frankly, I've drunk worse. And as the price of £2.49 a goblet actually works out at £9.96 a bottle, it *ought* to be drinkable.

There's something to be said when the means of delivery is less palatable than the wine itself. Yes, I could have poured the wine into a proper glass. Equally, if there was any merit in serving wine at home in flat-rimmed plastic receptacles, I could have poured decent wine into a yoghurt pot.

CONTAINMENT POLICY

What to do now with my plastic goblet? It says on their website that the goblet is 'in fact near unbreakable' which, as another offspring is fond of saying, sounds like a wager to me.

But on the base it says that you can 'reuse' it. The manufacturer's website seems devoid of suggestions, so if anyone has any ideas for reusing a plastic flat-rimmed goblet, I would be interested to hear them. And as one should say in December, enjoy your Christmas, although it may only involve this product if you are pursuing your festivities outdoors.

Or on a train.

IV

Tools of the Trade

The Decanter
PK

I have taken to decanting my wine of late. But this is not to improve its flavour; a lot of the cheaper stuff just dies a brief death in contact with the air. Nor is it to reduce my consumption, although finishing an elegant demi-carafe seems to complete a meal, and suppresses the urge to go and slump in front of the TV and polish off the rest of a bottle.

No, the decanting is simply to avoid the suspicious glances of my household, as yet another garish bottle featuring animals of the world, flora, fauna, ugly graphics and strange typefaces threatens to grace the dining table.

Mrs K and I take great pride in the presentation of our dining table. I don't go quite as far as one restaurant I visited before opening time, where a white-gloved *maître d'* went around the tables matching every place setting, to the centimetre, against a photograph. (But I if I could . . .)

We are not eating off crates. Our dining table does not look like a student flatshare. We take an Indian meal out of the foil trays in which it arrives.

And if you do take care with your choice and layout of crockery, cutlery and napery then surely you should be concerned about the look of the wine bottle you put in the centre of the table?

I am not alone in this. That great style icon Bryan Ferry, interviewed in the *Wall Street Journal*, objected to a wine illustrated with the rock that makes up the vineyard's *terroir*. 'I hate that,' he said. You hate the wine, asked the interviewer? 'No, the label,' he said. 'I can't drink a wine if it has an ugly label.'

Bryan Ferry and I are as one on this. (Sorry, can I just have the pleasure of repeating that sentence? 'Bryan Ferry and I are as one . . . ')

It's been shown by lots of controlled tastings that our judgement of a wine is influenced by things such as cost, name, reputation and, of course, label. And why not? Like the plating up of food, or the framing of a print, the presentation of something helps to shape our experience.

I believe that actually, we *do* judge books by their covers, which is why we have versions of *Harry Potter* in adult jackets, and why the novels by one author will often be redesigned to match the cover of his bestseller. So I get a little exercised with critics who insist that we should ignore the label on a bottle of wine. Appearances *count*.

And bold, garish labels are disturbingly childish on an adult drink. They are more suited to fizzy drinks than to wine. I wouldn't be tempted even if the contents of a garishly labelled bottle *were* delicious. It would reduce my dining table to the status of a children's party.

Fortunately I do have a couple of very nice decanters, which are a pleasure to use and look at. But even before I did, I have to admit that I would pour wine into anonymous bottles, rather than put ugly specimens on my table.

(The Nicolas *Petites Récoltes* range of *vin de pays* came in completely clear glass bottles from which one could easily soak off the cheap paper labels. In the days before I could afford a decanter, I used one of these to serve wine anonymously. I was trying to follow the minimalist designer John Pawson, who had recommended a Baccarat crystal decanter – which looks like a wine bottle, has the capacity of a wine bottle, will aerate your wine no better than a wine bottle, but costs £238. The Nicolas bottle was equally hopeless for aerating, of course, although the pouring from the original bottle would help – but it only costs £5.49. And unlike the Baccarat one, it initially comes conveniently filled with wine . . .)

And a decanter will, of course, genuinely improve some wines in flavour as well as appearance. I was forced to put one Shiraz into a decanter, simply because of its hideous label depicting (Why? *Why??*) a species of South African grass. Bryan Ferry would, I am sure, have agreed, although I doubt he drinks much wine costing £6.95.

From the bottle, it was a tight, unforgiving little wine. It left my mouth resembling a cat's anus. But decanted, and left a while, the tannins softened, the wine opened up, and it became richer, softer and altogether better than its price tag might suggest. Even Mrs K 'thought it was all right,' an approval rating neither its taste nor its appearance would have been likely to achieve straight out of the bottle.

A decanter won't solve everything. And let's face it, while you can decant a bottle of red, it's a little odd to decant your white (and harder to keep it cold), while only an idiot would try to serve a sparkling wine decanted.

But at least it does keep your wine anonymous, attractive and suitable for a civilised dining table. And while a decanter can't make a silk purse out of a sow's ear, it can sometimes retrieve a satisfying drink from a cat's anus.

The Paris Goblet
CJ

Three quid. That's what it cost. For a complete, 75cl bottle, entirely filled with red wine. It spoke to me at ASDA, not a place I normally find myself in, but I had to get some really cheap pillows and I saw this stuff and I couldn't take my eyes off it, so I grabbed two bottles, tucked the pillows under my oxter and lumbered off to the checkout looking (quite plainly) as if I were off in search of a park bench and a rain-free day.

Then I had qualms once I got home with my pauper's treasure. Three quid is not much for anything. The price of a Saturday newspaper is nudging that, likewise a chocolate brownie at a motorway services, a packet of shoe insoles is probably a bit more, a discount CD bought on impulse during a visit to a rotting British seaside resort is maybe a bit less . . . I mean, three quid is next to nothing. Did I really want to drink this stuff? Anyway, I brooded on it for a bit until I remembered a discussion I'd had with PK.

The gist of which was that he couldn't understand why anyone would dishonour a good wine by serving it in a cheap wine glass; whereas I didn't much care either way, the old Paris goblet having numerous virtues, including near-unbreakability, a comforting fit in the hand, good mouthful-to-contents ratio. But he went on about a good big glass being necessary to let the grog breathe and warm up and open out and tell its story to the drinker. So I said to myself that a really dodgy wine, if served in a decent glass, will be framed so effectively by its container that it'll taste like the Ribena of the gods.

Do we have any of those human-head-sized wine glasses with foot-long stems that smart people drink from nowadays? Of course not. If we ever did have them, they got broken long ago, trashed in the dishwasher or carelessly snapped by my delinquent fingers. But I poked around in a forgotten kitchen cupboard and what did I find but some pleasingly weighty Edwardian-looking things in cut glass or crystal, which I can only assume were given to us by someone because we quite obviously neither could nor would buy objects such as these, not in this lifetime.

So I poured ASDA into one of these Mrs Keppel glasses, while using a regulation Utility goblet as a control, let it settle/breathe/decompose for a few minutes, and took a swig.

My standards are low, but I have to say that even served in gleaming cut glass in a well-lit and temperate room, ASDA's Carracci was pretty challenging. Once I'd uncrossed my eyes and taken a reference sip from the Paris goblet – just in case the fancy glass had recently been washed in bleach or had a dead spider in the bottom – I decided that it tasted, essentially, of suede. It was disappointing. It was disappointing because I'd convinced myself that a £3 bottle was the answer to a prayer; and that even if it wasn't, I could re-invent the stuff, *Pygmalion*-style, by dressing it up and endowing it with a phoney accent. A shabby new world would then be mine for the asking.

But it wasn't. The wine tasted of suede all the way down to the bottom, whichever glass I drank it from. And I'd bought two bottles! Luckily, I palmed at least half of the second bottle off onto No. 1 son (who either didn't notice or couldn't be arsed to complain) and that dealt with the problem, such as it was. And the thing is, although this experiment was a bust, I still feel moved to try to find ways to deceive the senses by re-contextualising the drink. Already I am planning to decant the cheapest of beverages into baronial containers; consume it blindfolded; smoke while drinking; eat cheese before, during and after; glug straight from the bottle and out of unfamiliar receptacles (tea cups, ink bottles, Tupperware). The mind/body nexus is mutable and capable of being tricked.

The Riedel
Tasting Glass

PK

This post is something of a riposte, following CJ's remarks about wine glasses. What may have seemed to many like a casual, passing reference to 'human-head-sized wine glasses with foot-long stems that smart people drink from nowadays' is clearly a reference to my fabulous Riedel Sommelier's Bordeaux Grand Cru glass.

This magnificent example of the glassmaker's art is, indeed, five and a half times the size of CJ's puny Paris goblet. It is not, however, the size of a human head. Well, maybe a baby human. Or an adult mango.

However, I can do no better than quote from Riedel themselves: 'This glass, first created in 1959, is not a design gimmick but a precision instrument, developed to highlight the unique characteristics of the great wines of Bordeaux. The large bowl (capacity 30 oz) brings out the full depth of contemporary wines made from Cabernet Sauvignon, Cabernet Franc and Merlot.'

(And it will not get 'trashed in the dishwasher' because it won't fit *into* the dishwasher.)

I need only compare it to his wretched little Paris goblet, that hideous little tennis ball of a glass condemned by George Riedel himself as 'the enemy of wine'. A glass too thick and too small to enhance the flavour, too shallow and open to enhance the bouquet, and too mimsy to suggest generosity. Favourite of the hired caterer and the student party – and almost impossible to purchase nowadays.

(I kid you not; as I travelled downmarket, from John Lewis via Robert Dyas to Poundland, I still found it impossible to buy a Paris goblet. Eventually, Select and Save of Hammersmith offered me six for £3.99; if anyone wants the other five . . .)

The Riedel glass is, obviously, considerably larger. Five and a half times larger, in fact. Along with the enhanced enjoyment of my Bordeaux, I think I did imagine that, seated at the head of the table with my tasting glass, I would immediately appear a knowledgeable connoisseur and masterful *seigneur*.

However, the glass may also convey the impression that I am intending to drink around five and a half times as much as everybody else. Or to drink five and a half times faster. Or I may just look a bit of a knob, sitting at the head of the table with a glass the size of a coconut.

Anyway, this being *Sediment*, I cannot, as Riedel suggests, showcase 'majestically structured red wines in all their complexity and finesse'. Sadly, they are strangers to my table. But in all fairness to this 'precision instrument', I thought I had to find something that exhibited at least one of the 'unique characteristics of Bordeaux'. Which Le Fontegnac Bordeaux, £3.99 at Sainsburys, clearly does. It comes from Bordeaux.

Something told me, however, that this was not going to have the sustenance of such great clarets as 1947, 1961 or 1982. That something was, in fact, the back of the label. It says without a hint of shame, 'It is recommended that this wine be consumed within six months of purchase.'

So, one for the Paris goblet, then. An aroma of wood – not oak, which could be promising, but wood as in Colliers – a dank, dark kind of scent. Then a shallow, fruity flavour, climaxing with palate-clenching tannins. Altogether reminiscent in my mouth of a leaking biro.

Not, I imagine, the kind of description usually employed by enthusiastic sommeliers. Interestingly, the bouquet in their Riedel glass *was* immediately enhanced, presumably because the wine had room to breathe. (Room? It's got an entire *apartment*.)

But this was a *bad* thing. M. Riedel talks of his glass 'unpacking the various layers of bouquet and delivering a full spectrum of aromas'. I could feel my nasal hairs cringing.

When it came to taste, again I have to say that the wine was, marginally, improved – less punishing on the palate. But that was probably because, given the surface area of a CD, it could evaporate faster. The aftertaste was just as acrid.

Where does this leave us regarding CJ and his dodgy wine/ decent glass equation? Well, like an actor in a spotlight, a glass precision-engineered to highlight the quality of a wine will highlight poor quality too. And if I have got to suffer the indignity of drinking wine at £3.99 a bottle, I am not simultaneously risking ridicule by cradling it in a glass the size of a small bucket.

The Corkscrew

CJ

My old Screwpull corkscrew has finally given up the ghost. Since there are effectively only two working parts in a Screwpull this is as much as to say that the Teflon® has worn off the screw so that the knife-through-butter sensation I used to get when taking out a cork has degenerated into a nail-through-tarmac feeling, quite apart from the fact that the corks come out broken more often than they used to.

What to get as a replacement? Same again, no? Well, kind of, except that in the intervening years I have found something which I think is better than a Screwpull – an updated Waiter's Friend, with a nicely engineered double-action neck brace (you know, that little metal arm which hooks over the neck of the bottle to provide leverage) *and* (the killer feature) a bit of Teflon® on the screw to make it super simple to insinuate it into the cork. Advantages over the Screwpull being that you don't have drive the screw all the way through the cork to get it out (risking breakage, or a leaky cork when you re-cork the bottle) *and* you can get the thing out much quicker, because less time is spent on the Archimedes Screw as it elevates the cork into the air. With a bit of practice, an intact cork can be out in five seconds, that double-jointed lever doing all the work for you.

How do I know this? Because we have one. Trouble is, it lives on our boat where (believe you me) it has been a life-saver, and I can't bring myself to nick it and put an inferior substitute in its place. Do I actually *have* an inferior substitute, just supposing I found it in me to sink that bit lower on the moral scale? Yes, a twenty-first-century Waiter's Friend bought from John Lewis, where it looked great, no-slip rubber grip, nice brushed-metal finish: only problem being that my one has a crap screw and a lever arm which is as much use as a toothpick.

So it's off to the internet, where I assumed there would be only two choices of corkscrew available in this world (Screwpull or Waiter's Friend), given that for a corkscrew to be worth advertising at all it must be both simple to use and completely reliable, considering the high-stress situations in which it finds itself.

It turns out, however, that human ingenuity has really let itself run riot in the matter of corkscrews, giving us more ways to open a bottle than there are stains on a plumber's vest:

- You can get them with professional bar staff single-action levers.
- You can get them motorised.
- You can get them motorised *with one-hand operation.*
- You can get them with that old-fashioned both-arms-in-the-air double lever action (one of the very worst ways of getting a cork out, 95 per cent chance of a complete breakdown).
- You can get them as an attachment for an electric drill.
- You can get them brass-plated and wall-mounted.
- You can get a novelty Bill Clinton corkscrew (the screw

emerging from Bill's crotch, and I am not making this up).

- You can, unbelievably, still get that cork extractor that isn't a corkscrew at all, but two slim fingers of metal that slide down between the cork and the neck of the bottle, possibly a worse idea even than the arms-in-the-air corkscrew.

- You can get the wooden-handled moron's corkscrew – that *Flintstones* corkscrew that I think my mum still has – a shaped wooden grip and a metal screw that smashes any cork it meets into seventy tiny fragments.

- You can get a corkscrew that looks a bit like a tulip.

- You can get a corkscrew that looks like a moustache.

- You can get a corkscrew that looks like a parrot.

And so on, seemingly without end. In fact there were only two stupid ones that I *couldn't* find. One was that appalling all-wood dual-action thing we had to put up with in the Seventies – as PK reminded me – where one tap-shaped handle drove the screw into the cork, and a second one, set on a contra-rotating thread, drew the cork out. It looked as if it were made out of the leftovers of a ski chalet and no one ever knew how to work it. The other was the sort that pumped air into the bottle through a hypodermic needle, the air pressure slowly forcing the cork out from below and presumably adding a quick spritz to your first glassful of Gevrey-Chambertin. No sign of that either.

On the other hand, where were the groovy two-step Waiter's Friends + Teflon®? Where, even, was the basic Screwpull? Eventually I stumbled upon a sane part of the internet, with both sorts and, just to seal the deal, the prices of Screwpulls and Screwpull variations seemed to have gone through the roof, especially when all you're buying is two bits of plastic and a cheap metal thread, so that was my choice made for me: Waiter's Friend, with all the trimmings.

But wait: do I even need a new corkscrew, given that nearly all my wine comes out of a bottle with a screw top? Well, every now and then I do come across a delicious wine in a bottle with a cork, and I do think, every now and then, that I *might* need to open a bottle such as this again, sometime, just supposing my life takes a quite unexpected turn at some point in the near future. So, yes, it *is* necessary and I *will* get a new Waiter's Friend, and then all I will need is the remaining £15.99 to get a bottle of wine that justifies a cork in the first place.

The *Pichet*
PK

For the uninitiated, a *pichet* is like a carafe – but smaller. *Much* smaller. It contains just 250ml of wine, a third of a bottle, a quantity described by Mrs K as 'quite sufficient' and by me as: 'Thanks, that sample was fine, can I have the rest now, please?'

But I recently enjoyed a restaurant pre-theatre supper with my own *pichet* of red wine – pouring when I liked, pacing my consumption, and remaining awake throughout the performance it preceded. (That's the theatre, not the dessert.) So I thought I might try using one at home, to see if it had a similarly civilising effect upon drinking alone.

Whether 250ml is a suitable amount of wine to drink with one's meal is clearly a matter for debate. Some see food and drink working in a kind of quantitative harmony; others view the food as essentially providing ballast for some serious drinking.

Some bars and restaurants provide a glass of wine which is just 175ml, and one Italian in Covent Garden says on its list that 'a 125ml glass of wine is available on request', an absurdly small amount which might just accompany one of those Toytown minimalist starters, but would be absorbed by two mouthfuls of toad in the hole. I particularly like the way it's 'available on request', confirming that, like an inflatable cushion, it's something which you're slightly embarrassed to ask for in public. Where I come from, 125ml is not drinking, it's salivating.

I have always been a great fan myself of the half-bottle (375ml) for a meal. The problem is that half-bottles are usually relatively expensive. Take The Wine Society's claret, for example: £6.25 a bottle, £4.25 a half-bottle. Completely understandable, given packaging, transport and all the other factors which remain the same, but you don't have to be Einstein to work out that you're better off at home buying a full bottle and drinking it in two halves.

(Which is exactly what I do when Chelsea are playing on TV – buy a full bottle and drink it in two halves . . .)

If it was just a matter of measurement, you could get a stonking great glass, slosh in 375ml of wine, and get stuck in. But not a glass filled to the top, or else what Keats described as 'beaded bubbles winking at the brim' will inevitably be winking their way past that brim and down over the tablecloth. There must be a happy relationship between the wine and the air within a glass, which not only allows for swirling and aeration, but also accommodates the clumsy amongst us, and acknowledges that the greater the quantity of wine in one's stomach, the greater the quantity of ham in one's fist.

And the best way of maintaining that ideal quantity of wine in a glass is by topping it up, the act of pouring, which punctuates civilised eating and drinking like chapter headings in a novel. I somehow feel that the more often you pour, the more you feel you've drunk, as if the experience has been refreshed along with your glass. It's pouring from my *pichet* which I really enjoy; assessing, measuring, pacing each pour, the amount remaining clearly visible (unlike a bottle), and its solo character allowing you complete control, without intervention by waiter or wife. Pouring is one of those things that lifts supper alone above a simple act of refuelling. Better by far the glass modestly filled and frequently topped up, than the large one set before you like both a challenge and a constraint.

But while we're on the matter of constraint . . . It's a depressing fact that my *pichet*'s 250ml of wine, or 3.3 units, is precisely the daily NHS alcohol limit for men. Now, I have been deeply suspicious of these alcohol limits, ever since it was revealed by someone from the Royal College of Physicians that their original calculation, rather like a WMD dossier, was based on nothing more than 'a sort of intelligent guess'. However, I put it out there for what it's worth; if you use a *pichet*, you can fill it, look at it and think, well, according to the NHS, that's my lot. Look on, ye mighty, and despair.

Finally, the answers to some key questions:

No; thanks to the shape of this *pichet*, if you use it for white wine, it does not look too much like a urine sample.

No; even if I may look like one, when I'm sitting here alone, pouring out my own wine in this manner, I do not *feel* like a tosser.

Yes; it does create more washing-up.

Duralex Glasses

CJ

This news just in: throw away that Paris goblet and that crystal toilet bowl so beloved of PK. The answer to all your drinking needs is (of course!) the Duralex Picardie range of glassware.

Why has it taken me so long to acquire a pack of these miraculous tumblers? Was it some residual shame at those years of schoolboy smuttiness (*Durex*, ha ha, we said, given the thousands of them filling up the school dining hall)? Was it lack of opportunity? Was it laziness?

Almost certainly the last. But when I found a Picardie six-pack in a surprisingly snotty little shop in town, I knew that Destiny had sounded its trumpet and I had to get my fix of these stupendous vessels. So I bought an inital half-dozen, and the effect is every bit as magical as I'd anticipated. *Any* beverage tastes better – orange juice, tap water, whisky – while wines of all complexions are at last given that proper stage on which to express themselves.

The secret of Duralex's success? It's a tripartite strategy.

1) The faceted shape of the glass ensures plenty of flattish surfaces to press your sweating fingers against, thus ensuring a firm, steady, comforting grip at all times.

2) The 16cl version holds just the right amount for this writer, a couple of good swigs or four decorous sips before needing a refill.

3) It is virtually unbreakable, so if you chance to put it too close to the edge of the table, or just let go of the thing altogether, no harm done. Thus it penetrates the essence of the relationship between glass and drinker, which demands *reassurance*: the drink is precious, the pleasure is momentary and contingent, the dignity of the drinker is vulnerable, the situation is highly charged. The glass has to be not only an extension of one's senses, but at the same time provide confirmation of a differentiated, tangible reality standing apart from human uncertainties.

The Picardie is as close to perfect as I can imagine and once again, the French have found the answer to a question we English are scarcely aware of.

Tumblers

PK

Everywhere I look now, wine is being presented in tumblers. It's the *fashion*. So naturally, with my fashionable buttoned-up collar and bare ankles to the fore, I'm on the case.

There's a notion that serving wine in tumblers reflects something of European simplicity, of *cucina povera* and down-to-earth authenticity. Most photography of 'simple' food, shot against weathered boards or zinc tabletops, now has to be accompanied by wine in tumblers. The *Observer Food Monthly* (than which one cannot get more fashionable) is full of them. Nigel Slater has fallen prey.

Our local designer pizza restaurant (for yes, we live in the kind of locale which has one) provides tumblers for its challenging organic wine. And perhaps the biggest influence of all has been Polpo, a small and of course fashionable chain of London restaurants based on Venetian *bacaros*.

Now, CJ passionately extols the virtues of drinking wine from Duralex tumblers. He certainly doesn't claim that drinking wine from tumblers is fashionable. Not because it is or isn't, but because CJ does not concern himself with fashion. Nobody looking at CJ would say, now *there's* a slave to the catwalk.

So I ignored his enthusiasm, with the magisterial aloofness for which I am renowned. CJ, after all, is a chap for whom a tumbler represents the lesser of wine receptacle evils, descending from a Paris goblet to a mug.

And surely a tumbler is a rubbish glass from which to properly appreciate wine? It is too open, so you don't get a proper sense of the bouquet. It is too thick for subtle sipping. Its shape means that you can't really swirl with it; and the lack of a stem means you're forced to clutch it inelegantly in your fist like a grenade.

Polpo's owner, Russell Norman, says that serving wine in tumblers reflects a presentation which has 'no pretentious flourishes'. Of course, if everyone else uses wine glasses, if a wine glass is the norm, then a tumbler *is* a pretentious flourish, *n'est-ce pas*? And Polpo listed an Amarone at £67; is that an everyday wine to be slugged from tumblers?

But Norman goes further in proselytising the use of tumblers. 'I strongly recommend you try this at home, too,' he says in his Polpo cookbook. 'It gives the wine a lower status than perhaps you are used to if you dine in tableclothed restaurants, but I feel that this is right with humble food shared amongst friends. There is also something tactile and homely about a small peasant glass that you don't get with an expensive balloon.'

Try this at home, eh? Well, a few issues first. Point one; it is hard to give our wine at home a 'lower status' than it already has. Otherwise Lord Sainsbury would be *giving* it away.

Point two – can our table still be 'tableclothed', please? Or is it important for a 'homely' feel to expose its old stains, and that bit where the veneer got busted off?

Point three – could the food we share with friends *not* be described as 'humble'? I have found that phrases like 'terrific' are much more conducive to marital harmony.

I'm afraid I struggle with the idea of laying our dinner-party table with tumblers for wine. If anything, I am trying to *raise* the status of our wine when we share it with friends, not lower it. And fashionable our friends undoubtedly are, but presented with tumblers, half will have filled them with water before you could say *bacaro*. No, this 'small peasant glass' business only works if your friends are small peasants.

But what if it's just me and Mrs K, drinking young, bright wine with a simple supper? Suddenly, it begins to make sense.

We do not have the Duralex design classic tumblers. No, we have Pokal tumblers, which are *like* Duralex tumblers, in that way that things from Ikea are often *like* something else. But they are squarer, chunkier – more like those in Nigel Slater's photographs – and they are six for £2. That's 33p a glass, surely a very *povera* price. I don't know whether it's a factor in Polpo, but it's probably cheaper to smash them than to wash them up.

I fill them politely, halfway. This is not a lot of wine, and means you have to replenish it frequently, but that is itself a satisfying act. And the whole exercise seems to suit a simple lunch with simple wine, at home, with no guests.

And Mrs K agrees. She feels it is 'relaxed', that it's 'a sign that we know what we're doing'. It reflects, she thinks, the 'every-dayness' of drinking simple wine at home. All things of which I am in favour.

There is a satisfying degree of purpose about drinking wine from a tumbler. It lowers expectation; it promotes function over form. There is wine that does its job, but doesn't *deserve* a wine glass, in the way that a hot dog satisfies a hunger but doesn't deserve a plate. It seems somehow right to drink it from a tumbler.

And drinking wine out of tumblers gives you one further thing. A talking point.

V

Thinking and
Drinking (1)

Dinner at CJ's

CJ

PK is round at our house again, eating every piece of food he can lay his hands on while his wife is away, and this gives us a chance to talk arrant nonsense about a bottle of Château Liversan Haut-Médoc which he's brought round and about which he harbours reservations. Frankly, the stuff he has reservations about is between ten and fifteen times nicer than the stuff *I* have reservations about, including the bottle of Lidl Shiraz/Cabernet Sauvignon I have been keeping back specially in order to annoy him with, but still.

After a brief and embarrassing drinking encounter with the Lidl red, in the course of which we pull faces like two men stumbling upon an open grave, it's down to the Liversan. This allows us to remark with telling sagacity that its nose and elegant structure are tragically compromised by a fatal lack of *heft*.

'It lacks heft,' I say.

'Yes, it lacks heft,' says PK. 'It's somehow short on weight.'

'It should be weightier, shouldn't it?'

'I would have thought it ought to have more heft. I mean, it's a 2008. It shouldn't be running out of steam this early.'

105

'In another five years?'

'There'll be nothing left.'

'In five years, it'll have faded to nothing.'

'Such a shame.'

'It needs more heft.'

'More *power*,' PK says, clutching at the air with his free hand.

'Do you always talk about wine like this?' asks my wife, not bothering to disguise her incredulity.

'Yes,' I say. 'Yes, I think we do.'

Having decided that the Liversan, like a sketch by Watteau, is charming but in danger of disappearing into nothingness, we have a go at an ordinary Médoc that I have accidentally acquired.

'It's more robust,' PK announces, looking around to see if there's any more food.

'But lacks complexity,' I announce back.

'Definitely not as complex.'

'Not such a well-made wine.'

'Short on *finesse*.'

'Entertaining enough, in its way.'

'But short on *finesse*.'

'Are you looking for the cheese?'

'I might be.'

'It's quite engaging in a robust sort of way.'

'I mean, it would do at a pinch.'

'Plenty of fruit in the nose.'

'Surprisingly fruity nose.'

'But not much *finesse*.'

My wife attempts to put a stop to this by simultaneously rolling her eyes and making coffee, while I am struck by a pang of regret for the Lidl Shiraz/Cabernet Sauvignon, which I actually had hopes for in the way one might for an ugly but brave child. This is not least because some German Pinot Blanc I bought from Lidl at the same time turned out to be a bit of a bargain, nice floral notes, hint of caramel in the finish, a well-made white, I thought, and I was hoping to repeat the trick with my foul Australian red. *That*, I told myself, will be a blow for the revolution, a grenade straight through the palace windows. I look at the bottle of Australian red, willing its contents to taste nicer.

'You don't fancy a bit more of the Australian?'

'God, no. What's this? Is this Grappa?'

'We can't start on that.' I don't want to die, here, tonight. 'It's horrible, anyway.'

'I'm so disappointed by that Liversan. I've got another bottle at home, as well.'

'How many did you buy?'

'It was a special offer.'

'That Australian red could have been a contender.'

'I don't think it's worth hanging on to, now.'

'It's been open for a while. It might be worth another try.'

'It could have been very good. It very nearly *is* very good.'

'It didn't have to be good. It only had to be good enough to keep down.'

'Which was why it was on offer.'

'Now it's had a chance to breathe, I think it could work.'

'It's a pity.'

'It's a pity.'

We sit there, our silence only disturbed by the low hum of my wife's disapproval, and ponder our missed opportunities, as old men will do when they've had their hopes got up and nothing to show for it.

Quaffing and Glugging

PK

Am I a fool to want wine drinking to be something of a sophis-ticated activity? Was I naive to aspire, for all of those years, to a cellar, a carafe, a smidgen of knowledge and an appreciative sip? I only ask, because it seems that, even in relatively upmarket UK publications, drinking wine is now frequently described using two verbs – 'quaff' and 'glug' – which are redolent of frankly oafish consumption.

In just one trawl, I find that the *Telegraph* recommends enjoying 'a glug of vino'. In the *Independent*, you can 'glug' some natural wine, while a Cape blend is described as 'an affordable glugger'. The *FT* called respected winemaker Michel Chapoutier 'quaffable and quotable'. The *Spectator*, usually a bastion of tradition, refers to a Chardonnay as 'a real glugger'. And the *Guardian* says that 'Sometimes all you want is something light, crisp and quaffable' – well, *speak for yourself*.

There are other equally distasteful terms around; I felt forced to take a *Telegraph* wine critic to task, for 'swilling' and 'sluicing' her summer wines, which hardly makes them sound desirable. But 'quaff' and 'glug' are particularly widespread.

And Waitrose, perhaps England's most upmarket supermarket chain, has trumped the lot. In an issue of its *Waitrose Kitchen* print magazine, Olly Smith manages both. In a single issue, he directs us to 'glug' one wine, and to 'quaff' another.

What would be the food writing equivalent? 'Wolf this down for lunch'? 'Scoff this one for supper'? One really can't see Nigel Slater ending a recipe with 'Great to guzzle with friends'. But are the guests eating food any less oafish than the guests drinking wine?

Presumably these writers want to convey some kind of Falstaffian, Merrie Men bonhomie, with everyone waving goblets and tankards – but this is not the raucous scenario I believe Mrs K has in her mind's eye when we invite people round for dinner. Would *you* welcome a guest, and ask, 'Are you quaffing tonight?' Or pour a glass and say, 'Fancy a glug?' Our guests neither quaff nor glug; they sip and savour their wine, as they discuss high-minded matters and exchange witty *repartee*. (Although sometimes CJ does visit . . .)

Perhaps 'glugging' is also supposed to echo the sound of carefree pouring, like an arsonist waving a bottle of petrol about a room? Not in *our* house, I'm afraid, where guests tend to prefer their wine in their glass rather than their lap.

Easy drinking, that's what these writers want to suggest – and I'm afraid that's another of my *bêtes noires*. When is drinking *not* easy, for goodness sake? It's a reflex action! If you're finding that a wine is 'difficult' drinking, you don't need a wine critic, you need a doctor.

'Quaffing' often has a critical tone; celebrities or rich bastards always 'quaff' champagne, while proles like us simply drink it. Deconstruct *that*, Mr Waitrose. But I thought, in the interests of research, I should at least try to 'glug' a wine.

I therefore took a large mouthful of air in with my wine, and swallowed the lot with a kind of reverse belch. It certainly made an unattractive noise which could be described as 'glug', rather like the final emptying of a sink.

However, the result was also that a painful bolus of air descended my oesophagus with agonising slowness. This is what I imagine it must be like to swallow a golf ball. If any wine critic seriously thinks such 'glugging' is to be encouraged, I suggest they try this painful activity for themselves, and then think again.

And what happens when, instead of quaffing or glugging, you simply *drink* one of these wines? In a civilised manner, slowly and considerately, without sonic accompaniment from either bottle or digestive system?

One of Waitrose's vulgarly described offerings is the Tsantali Cabernet Sauvignon. This comes from the Greek region of Halkidiki, which I can't help thinking sounds like something R2D2 would say. A Greek cabernet sauvignon – when CJ heard what I was drinking, he said, 'I admire your moxie, kid.'

Whereas Olly Smith said, 'Quaff it with steak, chops and top-quality bangers.' Not sausages, you note, or even *loukaniki*; but 'bangers' . . .

Well, it's a competent, straightforward cabernet sauvignon; that slightly burnt aroma, but a bit flat in the mouth; a little brief resonance on the palate . . . but then gone. No richness, no complexity, no *grip*. Perfectly OK, and with a hefty 14.5 per cent alcohol, which will assist the goblet-waving; but for £9, I'm afraid I expect something a little more memorable.

But perhaps this is what it's really all about? Wine for people who don't want a stimulated palate getting in the way, slowing down the process of swallowing in large draughts (as Dr Johnson defined the verb 'to quaff')? In which case, why not go the whole hog, and provide alcohol via an intravenous drip?

THINKING AND DRINKING (1)

I shall not, in the foreseeable, be filling my guests' glasses with a hearty 'There you go, quaff that!' Nor inviting Olly Smith to demonstrate his glugging technique over our sink. Nor, indeed, purchasing another bottle of the unmemorable . . . what was it called?

Wine on a Boat

CJ

I'm on this sailboat, with the wife, grimly amusing myself off the south coast of England, and if there is one thing you think about when you're sailing and you're not absolutely certain you *like* sailing, then that thing is drink. And if you do not have a fifty-foot yacht with a really nice fridge and a gimballed wine rack, any drink you bring on board an elderly thirty-six-footer (to take a case in point) is going to get hurled around like medicine in a bottle, to say nothing of assuming that spectral haze of diesel which attaches itself to anything kept below decks for more than a day.

It calls for specialist knowledge to introduce a nice bottle of wine onto the boat and expect it to remain in good order for more than half an hour – a knowledge I do not have. Instead, whenever I go aboard, I poke around the various lockers to see what other people might have left behind in my absence, or go through the supermarket bags we have brought with us, in the hope that, even though I know I forgot to bring any wine with me, my memory might be faulty and, yes! Here's that bottle of indestructible Londis Red Burgundy my subconscious successfully gave house room to all those hours ago!

THINKING AND DRINKING (1)

So I go through this pantomime, like a child. This time, though, I find a bottle of rioja rolling around in a locker under the settee, which comes as a complete surprise to me, especially as it has a cork and a nicely prissy label. I cannot have bought it myself. Nor can I have bought the Brightwell Vineyard Oxford Rosé hiding in the partitioned booze holder in the centre of the saloon table. This turns out to be English and I believe that I've only ever drunk an English wine once in my entire life, a kind of fizzy white from Herefordshire, not unpleasant, mildly cleansing in fact, like a glass of Optrex with some gas bubbles in it. I look at the rosé doubtfully.

The fact is that on a boat you need beer for fine weather, and spirits for everything else, all the time. Cheap whisky is good (Tesco's, bought by the magnum) with a chaser of Calvados to administer that final blow to the back of the head at nightfall. All three drinks can take hours, months, of physical punishment and bilge water, and come up tasting fresh enough to take away the raw terror of sailing. Sometimes they're even better for being a bit salty.

And what do you know, the rioja has had it, and (even though I polish the whole bottle off with glowering determination) tastes too much of things like stamp adhesive and shoe polish to be much fun.

But the Brightwell Vineyard Oxford Rosé! I don't know who these people are, but after I've given the rosé some time in the boat's doughty old fridge, out comes this nicely blushing stuff, robust enough to withstand the aggressive neglect that happens in sailing, tasty enough to inspire nods towards *appley* and *somehow vanilla* and with a very tidy way of applying itself to the dead centre of the tongue before disappearing down the back of the throat without any of the *whoofs* and *barfs* that other rosés have a way of surprising you with.

113

And English too! I mean, given the thick-wittedness of most yachties, you can't be seen to be drinking rosé at any time, on account of effeminacy; but if you told them it was *British*, well, then, sentimental bigotry would take over and you'd be allowed to carry on. Who'd have thought it?

From Plonk to Plonkers

PK

It's uncanny. Like me, he began by drinking Mateus Rosé at the age of sixteen. Like me, he felt that 'The fact that wine had no place on my parents' suburban dining table seemed to confirm its consumption as a mark of sophistication.' Sadly, at that point, our wine writing careers diverged. Sadly, at any rate, for me.

The American author Jay McInerney has come a bit further, since a passing reference in his first novel, *Bright Lights, Big City*, where the narrator drinks wine that offers 'a bouquet with a hint of migrant-worker sweat'. His writing has allowed him to rise from drinking plonk to recommending a rosé champagne at $700 a bottle.

Not that he's necessarily *paying* that. He's now a celebrity writer, adding to his celebrated novels with a celebrated wine column in *House & Garden* and the *Wall Street Journal*, of which his book *The Juice* (Bloomsbury) is the third collection. He now gets invited to the vineyards, the châteaux, the restaurants and ultimately the big-ticket dinners, the 'bacchanalian gatherings' as he calls them, where he gets to drink the greatest wines in the world. And where he meets some truly awful people.

Given the chance, any of us might grab an opportunity to hobnob with VIPs, and drink their absurdly expensive wines for free. But while I have a great deal of interest in wine, I have little interest in the people who run its businesses. There may or may not have been a Mr Johnnie Walker, but meeting him would not alter my opinion of his whisky. I would simply ask him why he strode around looking like a tosser.

McInerney gains access to the rarest and most expensive wines of the world via a succession of individuals, whose careers, clothes, dropped names and luxurious lifestyles dominate this book. And they culminate in a repellent set of super-rich, willy-waving wine collectors, in a chapter appropriately entitled, 'His Magnum Is Bigger Than Yours'.

Now, we English have always been wary of the *arriviste* – or, in our popular contraction of the French term *nouveau riche*, the Noov – whose newly acquired wealth is displayed through the purchase of the most expensive items, without any commensurate knowledge or taste. (I fall into neither of these categories, as I am tragically aware of both my poverty and my ignorance.)

I'm reminded of the old tale of a Northern industrialist, visiting a top London restaurant to celebrate a commercial success. 'What's your most expensive wine?' he demanded of the waiter, without even opening the list.

Thinking of the legendary dessert wine, the waiter replied, 'That would be the Château d'Yquem, sir.'

'Right then, lad,' said the industrialist. 'We'll start with two bottles of that – and keep it coming!'

This was the kind of criticism levelled at a sports personality, when he foolishly revealed his taste in wine to the *Gazzetta dello Sport*. His list of expensive, trophy wines was immediately dismissed by the *Daily Telegraph* as 'the list of a labels man, who'll drink anything as long as it scores lots of points and costs a lot of money'.

'We're talking,' they went on, 'about someone with the taste of an insecure Russian oligarch.'

And this is the sort of company into which, as the prices of the wine rise, McInerney inevitably moves, until finally a chap wearing a 'windowpane sports jacket over an open white shirt showing plenty of chest hair' is sabering open a $10,000 bottle of 1945 Bollinger, before buying two bottles of rosé champagne at auction for $84,000.

We're a long way from plonk. This chap is 'Big Boy', a property magnate who, when asked by McInerney if his cellar might contain more than fifty thousand bottles, says 'Hell, I have fifty thousand bottles of '96 champagne!'

McInerney writes, 'I personally consumed, by my best estimate, over $20,000-worth of his wine – including the 1945 Mouton and the 1947 Cheval Blanc – and I was one of fourteen drinkers.' Well, lucky Jay; but given that 'Big Boy' provides the most disgusting sexual analogy for the tightness of a champagne that I have ever heard, he does not sound the kind of chap I would myself invite to High Table.

Personally, I would have liked to know how those extraordinary wines actually *tasted* . . . and while McInerney provides a fascinating insight into a number of wine people and their lifestyle, he is less good, to my mind, on describing their wine. His analogies are rooted in the world in which he is moving. If one Burgundy is 'a Ferrari' and another 'a Mercedes' – one champagne 'a Porsche 911 Carrera' and another 'the 911 Turbo' – I'm afraid I'm none the wiser.

The actual price of drinking these wines is not the sum for which they are auctioned, but the time you might have to spend with people who wear windowpane sports jackets, crocodile shoes, and sunglasses formerly owned by Elvis. Are *those* the 'marks of sophistication' Jay associated with wine back in his suburban youth? Perhaps that's why we diverged – because they certainly weren't mine.

I guess I'll stick with the plonk. McInerney can stick with the plonkers.

POSTSCRIPT

In that chapter, McInerney writes about a chap called Rudy Kurniawan, 'who vies with [Big Boy] for the Man with the Deepest Cellar title, and who's alleged to spend more than $1 million a month on wine . . . Rudy is widely believed to have had a major impact on the escalating prices of the fine wine market.' Indeed; in 2013, Rudy Kurniawan was found guilty of fraud by a federal jury, the first person to be tried and convicted of selling fake wine in the US. So who knows what some of those plonkers were actually drinking. Plonk?

Queen Victoria's Tipple
CJ

I am so bored that in desperation I re-open my copy of Kingsley Amis's *Everyday Drinking* ('the *New York Times* bestseller', it says on the front) and look for something to stimulate my jaded sensibilities. Kingsley Amis (unlike me and PK) was an acknowledged drink expert (whisky in particular) and pretty much a functioning alcoholic in everyday life – quite apart from being a well-known novelist, biographer and critic. The pieces that make up *Everyday Drinking* were originally written between 1971 and 1984, and if nothing else, give you a nice snapshot of upper-middle-class boozing habits forty years ago.

That said, Amis's idea of a well-stocked drinks cabinet, even allowing for the intercessions of time, sounds a bit of an acid trip. Apart from the mainstays of gin, whisky, vodka, etc., he recommends keeping: an orange liqueur; a cherry liqueur; Benedictine; Crème de Menthe; Crème de Cacao; orange bitters; a bottle of sugar syrup; and a selection of French *and* Italian vermouths. Christopher Hitchens reckoned Amis was 'a very slight cocktail bore', which might account for this terrible catalogue, but there you go: the Seventies were both stickier and more brightly coloured than the newsreels suggest.

On the other hand, he's bang on in his attitude to wine writers. He quotes a contemporary wine critic who was unwise enough to claim: 'Rather a jumbly, untidy sort of wine, with fruitiness shooting off one way, firmness another and body pushing about underneath. It will be as comfortable and comforting as the 1961 Nuits-St-Georges once it has pulled its ends in and settled down.' According to Amis, this kind of stuff 'receives a deeper and more educated contempt from real wine-drinkers than from the average man in the pub', but I'm not sure that time hasn't overtaken him and that, in this age of plenty, we're not all meant to be equally opinionated by-the-yard wine blowhards.

But on the other *other* hand, he has got this fantastic section on fatal-sounding drinks. Some are sensible enough (dry Martini; Manhattan), while others are plainly stupid. The Kingers (named for Kingsley Amis) contains montilla ('a lightly fortified wine from Spain'), orange juice and Angostura bitters. Queen Victoria's Tipple is simply half a tumbler of red wine + Scotch. Evelyn Waugh's Noonday Reviver is a (hefty) shot of gin, and half a pint of bottled Guinness, topped up with ginger beer.

It's the stupid ones that sound so appealing. And the one that appeals most is Queen Victoria's Tipple, a) because it's incredibly simple, b) because I have the ingredients to hand. Slight snag: it's only half past ten in the morning. How much Scotch to put in? Amis recommends 'stopping a good deal short of the top of the tumbler'. He also adds, 'Worth trying once.'

I get a really small Duralex tumbler, throw in some New Zealand Pinot Noir that someone brought with them to the house and which has been sitting around, half-drunk, for a couple of days, and then rather less than half as much again of Tesco's

Finest Special Reserve Scotch whisky. I stare at it, then forget that it's there and about three minutes later absently take a swig. Deadly mistake. It has a taste somewhere between thin gravy, treacle and a three-day-old bonfire, with a real chesty punch, like being hit in the sternum with a bag of sand. *It actually makes my eyes water*, and two sips later I am numb enough to have surgery. It is kind of fantastic, but it is not a drink. Queen Victoria was violently opposed to abstinence from alcohol, regarding it as a 'pernicious heresy'. Gladstone was appalled by this particular mixture, which was apparently her preferred dinner-table beverage. For once, he was right. The Old Queen, like Kingsley Amis, must have been shitfaced, most of the time.

Breakfast Wine

PK

Sometimes, you come across a concept of which the very linguistic construction suggests a potential shift in your lifestyle. It's like the first time you hear of onboard wi-fi, the staycation or slip-on shoes.

Thanks to an invitation from an importer, *Sediment* was invited to a tasting of some of Australia's premium wines; and there I heard Innocent Bystander winery, from the Yarra Valley, describe their sparkling Pink Moscato as 'a Sunday morning wine'.

It was like a revelation. I'm sure there are many differences between Sunday mornings in the Yarra Valley and those in London. But the mere notion of a 'Sunday morning wine' suddenly changed the whole prospect of waking up at the weekend.

Readers of a certain age will remember a television ad from the 1980s for the Halifax, which infected my generation with its smug notion of a loft-living lifestyle, 'easy like a Sunday morning'. And such a Sunday morning, with a Docklands apartment, cat, coffee, cool music and a crisp white shirt. Oh, and the only newspaper seller in London who is positively cheery in the morning, and is happy to accept notes from a cashpoint without responding, 'Ain't you got nuffink smaller, mate?'

But time moves on. You can tell that lifestyle's a thing of the past, if only because the chap in the ad gets his milk in a bottle. By now, he has hopefully found a more significant other than a cat to share his bed; and perhaps he has even progressed through the assault course years known as parenthood, during which mornings are anything but bloody 'easy', and through which he is unlikely to have retained yawning warehouse doors opening five floors up.

Personally, I always fancied Sunday mornings like those at Downton Abbey, descending to find a range of cooked dishes such as kedgeree lining the dining room under silver domes. For some reason, Mrs K hasn't quite got round to this provision. And my average Sunday morning begins, unlike the Earl of Grantham, by waking up with hair like Einstein, getting up before anyone else in my slumbering household and trudging downstairs to interpret the premises like a crime scene.

How many offspring and/or guests might be lurking in the bedrooms? What did they eat last night, and if the tins are anything to go by, how could it involve both tuna *and* baked beans? Are any bottles in the recycling and, if so, are they from the (acceptable) kitchen rack or the (forbidden) cellar? And is anything *meant* to be consumed at this time of day, like milk/bread/eggs/coffee, actually left in the house? Sadly, things here remain resolutely downtown rather than Downton.

So could a Sunday morning wine transport me from reality? (Of which, as we know, human kind cannot bear very much, and since waking I had tolerated at least half an hour.)

Innocent Bystander Pink Moscato is a gorgeous, flamingo pink, and comes in a cutely shaped half-bottle for about £6.95, with the all-or-nothing consumption that a crown cap (like a beer bottle) suggests. I'm immediately thinking verandahs, dappled morning sunlight, warm breeze, birdsong – *none of which*, it goes without saying, applied this week at our humble abode. Here in London it's rare to sit outside on a Sunday morning, and it's not my idea of fun to eat breakfast in a fleece, under a grey sky with drizzle in your muesli. No, to me that sounds too much like a music festival.

This wine is breathtakingly sweet, at a level that would normally make my teeth wince. But its crispness and effervescence keeps it light; it's like a Bellini made with strawberries, or a Buck's Fizz, but better. (Buck's is the only significant gentlemen's club to be founded since the First World War, and unlike most of the Pall Mall clubs I have visited, so very handy for the shops; but its great creation, Buck's Fizz, is surely fatally flawed by both its acidity, and its bits.)

The Pink Moscato is still 5.5 per cent alcohol, which puts it just a notch above Strongbow cider, and if someone came downstairs at 9 a.m. they would be rightly concerned to find me swigging from a can of Strongbow with breakfast.

But the half-bottle is just right for two. If person two actually gets up before you finish it . . .

Pink Moscato doesn't brighten the weather, but it does begin to brighten one's attitude towards it. It's just so much more *stylish* than a carton of fruit juice. I find myself feeling somehow celebratory, even reading the magazine section of the newspaper first. Things seem to be looking up, God's in his Heaven, all's right with the world . . . and yes indeed, the chap *does* arrive on time to clear out the gutters!

Plus, drinking wine at breakfast gets you out of some of the more irksome aspects of a Sunday morning. No, I can't drive to the supermarket, I'm probably over the limit. No, I shouldn't trim the hedge, I'm a trifle unsteady. No, that DIY involving the power drill may not be a good idea.

Oh, this is brilliant. I should probably go back to bed . . .

Drinking Alone

CJ

Fact: People who announce in a great gust of piety that *they never drink on their own* (usually giving you a look at the same time) are the worst sort of Puritan – the sort whose Puritanism derives from a psychological terror, i.e. that their own natures would compel them to drink the bottle dry and then the bottle after *that*, if there wasn't another individual around to stop them.

Fact: By reiterating their position constantly (and po-faced) they make it seem like the only responsible way to behave.

Fact: But the French drink on their own all the time.

Fact: Drinking on your own is a legitimate and intense pleasure, allowing you to brood on the mystery of life without having to explain your woozy philosophisings to anyone else.

Fact: It also allows you to drink stuff you otherwise wouldn't be able to drink in company, or would, at least, have difficulty accounting for. I recently reached an accommodation with a particularly scary dirt-cheap Chenin Blanc/Chardonnay/Sémillon, the usual mixture of a mouthful of ball bearings/escaped coal gas/rumour of incipient migraine, but still okay if you kept it almost frozen. Best of all, it was not just cheap but free, donated by my wife as a leftover from work. Not, though, a wine I would want anyone else to know about.

Fact: One of the most pleasurable things you can do, at any age, even better perhaps than just drinking a glass of wine, is sit in a quiet bar, on your own, with a glass of wine *and a cigarette* and achieve a state of Zen-like calm as the world goes on around you. Nowadays excessively difficult to achieve anywhere in Europe (and impossible in the UK), it marries Fact no. 4 above with the joy of a thoughtful cig in what Richard Klein calls 'a caesura in time'. Actually, he doesn't stipulate the booze, but in his magisterial book *Cigarettes Are Sublime* – an investigation of the cultural centrality of fag-smoking – he talks about the way a tranquil smoke can arrest time, freeing the smoker from the jabbering torment of ambition, human relationships, existential despair, etc. In this caesura, this intentional breakage of the flow, the contemplative stillness, is bliss.

Fact: *Cigarettes Are Sublime*, along with *Dieting Makes You Fat*, by Geoffrey Cannon and Hetty Einzig, are the two most influential books I possess.

Fact: Now I think about it, I probably drink *less* when I'm on my own. There comes a point where another glassful will invariably mean intoxication, and being *drunk* on your own is the living end unless you really, really want to be drunk (bankruptcy, doomed relationship, terminal illness). Whereas, when I drink with, say, PK, it's all too easy (PK having the capacity and persistence of a wet & dry vacuum) to try to keep up, thereby plunging heedlessly into that second or even third bottle, with appalling consequences. Whereas the act of putting the screw cap back on the unfinished bottle gives one a little thrill of maturity, as well as being an implicit riposte to Fact no. 1.

Fact: Which means I'm starting to *sound* like no. 1 and therefore must

Stop.

Nostalgia – Beaujolais Nouveau

PK

I wouldn't even have known it was Beaujolais Nouveau Day, had I not seen a chalkboard announcing it outside a pub. I wasn't aware of races to bring back this first wine of the vintage from France, or of parties to sample it; the whole experience seems to me rooted in a nostalgic era of wine bars with names like Champers. But once I'd seen it, I felt I had to try it out again.

(Distressingly, I did actually *find* a wine bar called Champers after writing that paragraph. Located in the prime suburbia of Eastcote, its orthographically challenged website proudly declares this wine bar to be 'as cosially electric as they come', a claim I genuinely cannot comprehend.)

Now, I'm not really in favour of chaps drinking wine in pubs. The thing is, a proper pint of real ale is something you can *only* drink in a pub, and it is such a wonderful thing that it should be linked, indissolubly, to drinking in pubs themselves. A pub that does not have draught beer is not a pub; it's a bar.

Wine in pubs, on the other hand, suffers from limited choice,

129

seemingly driven by economics rather than taste; and a painful mark-up, which means a single glass in a pub often costs as much as an entire bottle of the same wine from a shop.

However, in a rare experience for me, I was actually disappointed before I had even tasted this wine – because they weren't selling it by the glass. You had to buy a bottle.

I observed that this was not a sales tactic they were employing with, for example, gin. And I suppose I could have argued the toss with the landlord, but in my experience arguing with pub landlords is rarely a good idea. There are few debating chambers in the world's democracies from which you can be ejected on the grounds of your attitude, but the public bar is one of them.

In some ways, though, it made sense. Because Beaujolais Nouveau was never a wine to sit and savour by yourself. One label actually says that it's 'ideal to share with friends and family'. It's a sort of party experience, an occasion where you all agree it's a bit of fun, a bit of a lark, to try this barely drinkable wine, and the focus is really on going out with your mates. And if you all then agree that it tastes horrible, that's just part of the fun. Isn't it?

Anyway, I did not intend sitting on my own in a pub, nursing an entire bottle of wine, and lowering yet further the tragic image of *Sediment*'s authors.

Yet finding a bottle to take home and taste proved rather difficult. When I stuck my head into the nice wine merchants down the road and asked if they were selling it, they shook their head at me with that tolerant smile one employs to pacify a lunatic.

Because, of course, nowadays even the casual customer knows a bit more about wine than they did when this event took off back in the Seventies and Eighties. We are now used to being sold wines that taste acceptable whenever they are made. The new French vintage means less to us than ever; and whatever the occasion, we do not expect a merchant to sell us wine which tastes unpleasant.

Finally, in Waitrose, I found the Beaujolais Nouveau from Georges Duboeuf, the chap who has been most responsible for the international marketing of this event. His garishly coloured bottle is presumably intended to evoke the lively nature of both the wine and the occasion, while the back label talks of 'Beaujolais and French tradition', although it's unclear how this equates with a plastic cork.

Beaujolais Nouveau is released in November, and there's nothing you want quite so much on a freezing November night as a glass of chilled red. With temperatures so low, the bottle's conveniently chilled just by carrying it back from the store.

Do they recommend drinking this chilled because it numbs the palate? Because, as if you needed telling, it's pretty nasty. Its thin colour and spritely nose lead on to a real collision in the mouth between a tart body and that notorious bubblegum fruitiness on top. Perhaps if you had a single quick glass, from a bottle shared with friends, it might be tolerable, but its fruit evaporates quickly to leave a ghostly, inky-flavoured wine.

Perhaps we should employ the same gimmick in reverse? Perhaps we should ship over to France our very first birds shot on the Twelfth of August, before they've had a chance to hang? Scotch whisky, before it's matured? Or the very first Christmas puddings, before they've had an opportunity to steep?

Or perhaps we should nip out on the Metropolitan Line to suburbia, to enjoy our Beaujolais Nouveau in a wine bar like Champers, 'A legendry [*sic*] meeting place for all, for intimate chat, maybe watch some football.' Because those two activities go together so well.

VI

CJ's French Connections

Buying in Bulk
CJ

As a rule, whenever I buy wine, I march robotically over to the booze section of the supermarket, stand in front of hundreds of special offers and bargain disasters for about thirty seconds, then reach out in a trance and grab the first bottle that costs about £5. That's it. Everything after that is destiny.

There is, I know, a grown-up way of acquiring drink, which is to work out your preferences beforehand then buy in bulk, a couple of cases at a time, and work your way through the contents. I have two problems with this. First, I can never remember what I like, or if, indeed, I actually like *anything*. Second is that even if I can think of something that might be worth drinking, whenever this household orders even the most pitiable single case of wine, something goes wrong with the delivery.

Our experience with Tesco is a case in point, having managed four deliveries to our house, out of which no fewer than three were monumental cock-ups. But it's not just them. The wife rather daringly went to popular winesellers Laithwaites to order a case of my pa-in-law's favourite wine and have it sent direct to

135

his address as a Christmas present. Fine, the stuff turned up. But the pa-in-law already had an account with Laithwaites, so they billed him for his own present, instead of billing my wife. She called them up, explained, they said of course, we'll sort it out. What happened? Next time my pa-in-law put in for an order of his own wine, my wife got billed for it and he didn't. This makes no sense. They don't have the same names, they don't live in the same part of the country, they don't share credit cards. How can this happen?

Buying in bulk in person doesn't work much better. The original Oddbins chain would sell you plenty of stuff in one go, but it tasted terrible. My most recent visit to a *cave* in the south of France was so frosty that I ended up buying nothing at all. And I can't be arsed to get down to the nearest Majestic wine store (all of half a mile away) because the parking's rubbish.

Nevertheless, in a last throw of the dice, I have been tormenting myself with the thought of going to France on a day trip, buying a load of cheap grog and bringing it back in the car. Ever since the pound collapsed against the Euro a few years ago, the idea of the booze cruise has slightly tanked, but then my brother-in-law, who has an almost obsessional interest in doubtful bargains, started explaining about some outfit that covers the cost of your ferry ticket provided you buy £200 or more of booze, or at least they give you a voucher for the next time you cross.

Actually, just looking at it now, in black and white, I can see what a terrible idea this is, involving the purchase of a huge amount of wine I can't afford, plus fuel expenditure, plus the certainty that when I get my £200 of drink back home, it will turn out to be every bit as awful as the stuff I buy from the supermarket. And my car's falling to pieces, so I probably won't even make it as far as Dover.

There must be some way round this. Perhaps I should try

to get PK in on the scheme, not least because he has a newish executive-style saloon which won't break down on the M20.

The drawback with *that* is that he'll insist on high-end purchases such as cellophane-wrapped ham rolls on the ferry. When we get to the outlet in Calais, he'll want bottles of wine that have dates on them. Plus one of those terrible, terrible bourgeois restaurant meals you get all over France where the food tastes of mud and the service is medievally bad and it costs a fortune. 'Thus losing a significant percentage of what you have just saved,' as my bro-in-law (who used to be a finance director) observes.

Look: I just want enough everyday Shiraz, from almost any country, to be able to bathe in. Is that so unreasonable?

A Case from France Pt I

CJ

A development: my brother-in-law is set to go on one of his cross-Channel dashes in search of drink, and very kindly asks if he can get anything for me while he's there. *There* being the Calais Wine Superstore, chosen by him not least because it is strong on New World wines, his kind of wine, and also because they have given him a free ferry ticket for himself, his partner, and his car. If there is the tiniest inconvenience in this deal, it is merely that he has to go in mid-January, and a Severe Gale Force 9 is forecast.

The only other inconvenience, or at least it would be an inconvenience to me, is having to work out how much drink to buy in order to maximise the differential in duty between French and English prices, as well as make enough of a turn on it to cover the cost of the petrol. But this is easy for him, because he is a financial wizard, such a wizard that he actually aims to save about £300 net by getting his drink this way.

Off he goes in the severe gale, but both he and P&O are made of the right stuff, and the Force 9 blows fruitlessly, and he returns with the booze and his partner and the car headlights pointing at forty-five degrees up into the night sky on account of the incredible quantity of drink in the back.

And what has he bought on my behalf? Well, I had a quick scan of the Calais Wine website before he left and succumbed to the old tendency: in other words, I dived straight to the bottom as if I was trying to salvage a Mediterranean wreck, and found a generic Côtes du Rhône going for an eye-wateringly sensible £2.69 a bottle. Usual cockamamie reasoning: at this price, it doesn't matter what it tastes like; I'm the only one drinking it; if it doesn't kill me, I'm ahead of the game; I can always use it for fence paint.

Get me some of that, I said. My bro-in-law thought he could squeeze in half a case.

Now, as it turns out, he has been able to squeeze in a whole case, which is extremely decent of him, only for me, alarm bells are starting to ring. It is not exactly a question of retrospectively being careful what you wish for, but something like that. Six bottles of poisonous crap I can deal with, if indeed it turns out to be poisonous crap. Twelve bottles, on the other hand, are a bit more of a burden, a bit more difficult to get rid of, even if they do cost the same as a single bottle of good wine, even if they cost virtually nothing. How many chicken stews will twelve bottles make? How many marinades? How many solitary tussles with my liver will I have to endure? The stuff will be hanging around forever, like a curse.

Still. It comes in a nice bottle with a cork, and certainly looks the part. In fact it looks almost as good as a Saint-Émilion Grand Cru which I once drank, so that's promising. And the cork comes out okay, too, not something you can always take for granted at this level.

The taste, though, the taste. Straight off the bat, there seems to be no nose, and no finish. In the middle, however, there's a disturbing amount of action, involving a tangled blackberry sensation, some sandpaper, and most worrying, an invisible chemical gas I can't put a name to, the kind of smell that comes out of a car body shop or the duty-free section of an airport in the tropics. I start to fret that it, whatever it is, might blind me or cause brain damage. So I cork the bottle up again and leave it for a good six hours.

By evening, it's calmed down enough to drink without hurting, and, paired with some really aggressive Italian cheese, it could almost be wine, with a personality oscillating wildly between Sid James and Rutger Hauer. And in the morning, I feel no lingering effects beyond the usual ones of age and alcohol. So I think we can get through this. The lesson learned being to let the stuff breathe for about half a day before drinking. And keep the windows open. And probably not attempt more than one bottle a month. And choose more wisely the next time someone offers a helping hand. And, now I think about it, I might as well update my will, just in case.

A Case from France Pt II

CJ

The stuff I unwisely acquired courtesy of my brother-in-law is still with us. I've worked out that the least worst way to get through a bottle is to let it breathe for a day and take the first glassful very cautiously indeed. On this basis I have managed to eliminate a couple from the gaudy heap in the kitchen, only it doesn't seem to matter how many I dispose of, the same number of untouched bottles always seems to remain, lying in wait for me. Either I'm trapped in a tale of the occult, a W. W. Jacobs story, or something by Conan Doyle, or for that matter a variation on *The Sorcerer's Apprentice*, or it's guerrilla warfare, in which the kitchen has become French Indo-China and I am forever swatting back the forces of the Viet Minh only to see them regroup in larger numbers in a slightly different part of the wine rack. It is not a good way to be.

I Google *what to do with a lot of really bad wine*, which turns up some interesting suggestions. *Make casseroles with it* is an obvious one, but *turn it into sangria* rings the changes, as does *bathe in it* (it's vinotherapy, and keeps your skin supple), *use it as dye* (for that artisanal look), *add it to the compost*, or *make it into wine jelly.* Interesting but somehow not persuasive. And not close enough to just drinking it, which is the circle I want to square. The tragedy (it now appears) is that my filthy CDR is not white. Had it been white, it would at least have allowed me to chuck in some Crème de Cassis or Noix to adulterate the taste and get through it that way.

Sullenly I open a bottle of Minervois, bought from somewhere, a supermarket probably, to take my mind off things. Only to discover that the mainstream Minervois is *almost as repulsive as the CDR*. Why should this be? But before I have time to query the testimony of my own senses, the ground opens up beneath my feet and Hell gapes as I realise that *this* is the way the story is unfolding: all my other reds now taste as bad as the CDR and will *continue* to taste as bad, until I finish off the CDR – *which I can never do.*

There is only one thing for it: I must give up drinking wine. Given the sort of wine I usually consume, this will, God knows, not be much of a hardship. And to take its place? Whisky, of course. The wife gave up still wines long ago, but loves her Scotch (although not so much her Irish, and not at all her Bourbon) and it has to be said that although we've drunk some fairly shabby whiskies around the world, very few have been too revolting to keep down.

The only one I can recall – in fact, the only whisky which we couldn't stomach in any combination – was some stuff we got in Cairo a few years ago. We kept the bottle as a souvenir. The label – bearing a tantalising similarity to the famous J&B logo – announces the contents as *MARCEL A BLWND* [*sic*] *OF THE SUPER OLD DRINK EGYPTION*, which is not only a *Porduct of Egypt* but also *BRODUSET AND BATTLED BY THE SAMIOS*

COMPANY. Sadly, Egypt – a miraculous country in so many other ways – is not a great whisky-producing nation. Whatever went into the Marcel – grain? grape skins? potatoes? – came out as a kind of marsh gas in thin syrup, undrinkable with still water, fizzy water, or even Coke. Which I suppose is an achievement in its own right.

Marcel aside, I see blue skies and calm seas ahead, in my new whisky-only regime. A nice Speyside for special occasions; a supermarket blend for everyday. Plenty of ice in hot weather, and a mere splash of water in the winter months. Why didn't I think of this before?

Unless, of course, this is just another twist in the plot. Man forswears wine, takes to whisky instead. Whisky slowly begins to taste like Marcel, whatever its provenance. Man moves on to gin, brandy, vodka, beer. They all become undrinkable. Slivovitz, kümmel, arrack, rum, mezcal and absinthe all take their turns, every one of them doomed. In desperation, he resorts to tea and coffee, cocoa and even drinking chocolate, sometimes laced with rubbing alcohol, sometimes straight: same result. Soon, tap water is all that's left, but when he cannot keep that down, he dies of thirst, the last thing he sees being the mocking labels of the oh-so-affordable Côtes du Rhône he acquired at the beginning of the story.

Where did he go wrong? Are the gods of wine-drinking punishing him for presuming to get away with a drinkable wine at a bargain price? Was there an essential flaw in his character that led him to his destruction? Could we all learn from this? And was it wise, in the first instance, to get the stuff from an outlet called the *Satanic Wine Warehouse*?

A Case from France Pt III
CJ

The Côtes du Rhône is *still* here, although things have moved on in the last fortnight. First, I have managed to offload a bit by covertly dishing it up to people seated at our kitchen table (we don't have *guests* like PK, just people who turn up and consume; the last one stayed eight hours, polishing off a full lunch *and* a light supper) and feigning ignorance when they notice how horrible their wine is.

Secondly, readers of the *Sediment* blog pitched in with advice as to how to get through the stuff unharmed. One recalled his grandfather – in South Australia, some decades ago – blending 'various varieties for better balance. Sweet Syrah is cheap and can "fix" thin Pinot. Bitter tannins can be eased with Merlot.' While admitting that 'it's not always successful', at least 'we've had some acceptable outcomes'. I tucked this behind my ear for later, at the same time concurring with a reader called Anonymous who reminded me that 'mulled wine tastes filthy, so it doesn't matter what you make it with', while respectfully noting the opinion of another Anonymous, whose father had a penchant for what he called 'tank car wine', and whose trick with this terrible grog was to 'dilute with water or ginger ale and drink with food'. Someone else thought that I was being excessively faint-hearted about the Crème de Cassis and reckoned I should 'chuck it in ANYWAY . . . you'd be hard pushed to make the stuff worse than it already is, but you might just end up with something that tastes like a slightly sweet version of a New World cabernet blend.'

Deborah (no surname) suggested that I should 'take a bottle each time you go to a party or larger gathering where it can get lost among the other wines and nobody knows who brought it', which is of course one of the most practical solutions; while LondonPerson went off at a tangent over the Egyptian whisky, revealing, frighteningly, that 'Knockoffs and Zibib liquors can be made by mixing cheap sugars, corn or pomace with yeast, extracting the alcohol with a little pressure cooker, and then filtering it through a T-shirt or cloth.' And a mate of mine rang up even more tangentially to suggest that I should try mixing port and Guinness as a kind of all-purpose wholly corrupted alcoholic drink which will serve in any situation.

If there was a theme emerging, it involved admixture. As chance would have it, I was admixing only the other weekend at a birthday party. It was late and – speaking candidly – we were all slightly the worse for wear, when someone said, *Let's put the Sauternes in the champagne and see what happens*. So we did, about half and half, drank it and, so relaxed were we, we pronounced it good. Sweet, effervescent, an aesthete's version of Red Bull. In retrospect it was disgusting, but at the time the mood carried us over. At any rate, mixing was on my mind.

To warm up, I actually did the port and Guinness thing: not as bad as I'd feared, a bit like an old-fashioned porter rather than an extra stout, and with a delightful pinkish blush on the head. On the other hand, it wasn't so nice that I'd ever want to drink it again, so I moved on to the CDR. PK's argument was that, since the CDR was probably Grenache, Syrah and Mourvèdre in some combination, + or − and/or, I should buy a *reasonable* bottle of one of these and chuck it in to improve the blend. Ten minutes of deliberation at Waitrose saw me emerge with a Grenache costing almost three times as much as the original CDR, and wondering, actually, shouldn't I have got a Syrah (there was no Mourvèdre) given that the CDR was probably quite Grenache-packed already, and I might just be compounding the felony? Or better yet, a quite unrelated wine, a Merlot, maybe, just for the taste, and forget about following the recipe?

Too late. I mixed the CDR in with the allegedly decent Grenache, a ratio of about two to one. Took a swig. The same chemical haze, finish a bit like barbecue lighter fluid, slightly less psychotic in the middle, but not really an improvement. I tried the Grenache on its own, just to make sure: started well, spicy, hint of chocolate, followed by a so-so middle and an industrial conclusion. Then I went back to the CDR: still appalling. Months of trial and error would probably have yielded a better result, but as a one-off experiment, it was inconclusive; added to which, jumbling up Guinness, port and bargain Côtes du Rhône, is, frankly, a hangover in a bucket, and not a good idea.

It was only later, mildly detoxed, when I discovered a bottle of The Wine Society's White Burgundy, and unthinkingly took a sip, that I realised how Fate operates: disillusioned by my experiments in blending and depressed by my immovable CDR, I'd resigned myself once again to life as a third-rate wine drinker – only to find that my glass contained something fragrant, buttery, shapely, really delicious. There *was* drinkable wine in the world, and I had some. I practically cried with gratitude.

Cubi Filled by Pump

CJ

Hold the front page. I have seen the future and it is *nothing to do* with ultra-cheap bottled wines, but comes in a five-litre plastic flagon, filled by a man using a petrol pump.

This is serious. There we were down in the Ventoux, and it was Saturday morning, and what do the locals do on a Saturday morning in that part of the world but drive to their friendly neighbourhood *cave* to stock up for the weekend? So we did that, only instead of the grim trudge that accompanies a trip to (say) Majestic Wine – the trolley squeaking across the chill concrete, the haggard bankers and lawyers bracing themselves for that next dinner-party – at a *cave* called Terra Ventoux we found a barely supressed excitement, a mood both carefree and impossibly eager.

Why? Because of this man with the pump. Don't be put off – there was nothing dubious or furtive about the *cave* or the pump, or, indeed, the man. In fact the place was exemplary in its cleanliness, its bourgeois dignity. High-ceilinged, thronged with bottles of red and white (their take on the local Ventoux variety), panelled with sober brown woodwork, somewhere in atmosphere between a gentleman's smoking room and a sauna, everything about it said dignity and composure. But then there were these huge wooden vats, lined up against a wall, each with its own petrol pump. And, turn and turn about, with a pair of Frenchmen, one on the end of the pump hose, pouring the wine, the other standing contentedly over his plastic flagon like a dog-owner giving his pet a treat.

Because the majority of punters were arriving with their own flagons for a refill. Costing €2 and holding five litres, these *cubis* come with a plastic tap and a convenient carry handle, and will last a lifetime, or a year at least. The booze that flows in? The same as the stuff being sold, bottled and labelled, for €5 a bottle and rising, on the other side of the *cave*. How much do you pay for the plastic flagon version? A truly magical €1.35 a litre, plus TVA. That is not a typographical error: €1.35 a litre, or €6.75 the flagon. Of wine which, I can proudly report, is light, refreshing, stylish, well-balanced, and which slips down so readily it's almost impossible not to drink at any time of the day or night. I can't tell you how excited I was, watching my own *cubi* bubble up with the good stuff, knowing that I was now part of a great and profoundly civilizing ritual; and that I could remain very slightly drunk for as long as I wanted.

The only snag is the keeping. Lots of French customers were buying this same delicious wine in *BiBs* (Bags in Boxes), which keep the booze in a collapsible plastic vacuum bag so that it doesn't spoil over time through contact with the air. Not possible of course in a rigid *cubi*. So the intelligent *cubi* drinker takes his *cubi* home and straightaway decants most of its contents into old wine bottles that he then corks up again, thus minimising the air/spoilage interface.

I fully made a mental note to do this as I watched my *cubi* fill, but, once back at base, was so distracted by the incredible and unfamiliar bounty now sitting in my kitchen that I forgot to do any such thing until I was at least half-way through the flagon.

Opinions are mixed as to how long flagon grog can be expected to keep, given considerate treatment as opposed to damp-palmed bibulous neglect. A month to six weeks was a rough consensus. Suddenly and belatedly waking up to this problem, I realised that I had left it too late to decant and that the only thing to do was to drink with steady and increasing efficiency through the remaining wine before it had a chance to go off. This I am continuing to do, and although my Terra Ventoux is suffering a bit, it gamely refuses to die on me. Frankly, at €1.35 +TVA a litre, I would drink it even if it tasted like hair restorer. Every palatable sip between now and that state is a miraculous bonus.

A Tanker of Wine
CJ

I'm having a drink with a pal who is normally something of a genius when it comes to original and creative thinking, and the pal says, this is what *Sediment* needs: we need to acquire a small tanker, or bowser, drive it down to the South of France, fill it full of rough red wine, the sort that retails down there at 50p a litre, drive it all the way back to England, turn up at one of the many farmers' markets you find in and around London, and sell the contents of the bowser at 50p a litre + transport costs, piping it into the customers' own receptacles through a petrol hose, just like that Terra Ventoux.

'It can't fail,' he says. 'It is 100 per cent guaranteed success.'

As ideas go, I reply, this is less terrible than his other idea of building a novelty bubble car in the shape of an inverted Paris wine goblet, and driving it through the vineyards of Burgundy as a promotional tool, but only just.

'No, no,' he says, 'you're not seeing the full potential. Just think, the customer brings a plastic bottle, or flagon, to the farmers' market, and gets it filled up with authentic cheap red wine at an authentic price. How desirable is that? Maybe by a guy wearing a stripy vest and a beret.'

151

On a spectrum of terribleness, in fact, I would put it on a par with PK's now-discarded plan to launch the *Sediment* Roadshow, a kind of rock'n'roll wine tour ('Hallo, Oswestry!') in which PK and I charge an audience money to drink taster samples of bad wine, which we then disparage from the stage, amid bright lights and possibly dry ice. It has taken me a year to convince PK that I would rather eat loft insulation than submit to such an ordeal, but just writing it down, now, will probably set him off again.

'All you do,' continues the pal, 'is buy the stuff in sufficient quantity. You can't lose.'

I point out that the moment the bowser crosses the Channel, it will attract an eye-watering level of duty, which will instant-aneously wipe out the bargain-basement advantage the grog originally enjoyed. Assuming, that is, it's survived the 700-mile drive, swilling about in a stainless steel container like the contents of a cement truck.

He wrinkles his brow, as another insight comes in to land. 'No, you don't want a metal tanker. You want an actual oak wine vat, a really huge one, with *Sediment* painted on the side, attached to the back of the truck. People are going to queue up. The moment they see the huge vat, with the Frenchman in the vest, they'll start queuing. You could hire a Frenchman, a real one.'

But the staves of the barrel will move as the thing bounces over potholes, and the wine will leak out, and the Frenchman will be quite expensive in his own right, I say, not knowing why I'm even trying to rebut the concept – which seems to have acquired a life of its own, a Golem idea that cannot be killed.

'And the petrol hose coming out of it.'

There must be something about wine itself – some profound sense that it is not, still, quite culturally routine enough to be simply taken or left, used or not used, that draws the twitching hand of novelty towards it. I cannot believe that anyone would direct the same energetic whimsicality to grapefruit juice, say, or potatoes. Wine is still, at base, such an alien thing that it needs crazy repackaging, or off-the-wall tasting encounters, or special train journeys through wine-producing regions, or madcap stunts at farmers' markets, just to break through the otherness of it all.

But there it is. My fortune is going to be made by a huge, mobile barrel of undrinkable and overpriced red wine with a spreading puddle beneath it, served through a petrol hose by a comedy Frenchman, into washed-out two-litre Coke bottles, and bought by people who can readily afford good, drinkable wines, properly presented in glass bottles with labels.

'If you can't see it,' he says, 'you're mad.'

VII

PK's English Aspirations

Laying Wine Down
PK

This is about *not* drinking Château Léoville-Barton 1989. Readers unfamiliar with *Sediment*, and its somewhat idiosyncratic approach to wine writing, may well observe that there are probably thousands of wines I could write about *not* drinking. But bear with me.

I was recently taken aback by a statement on an American wine website which said: 'Fact is, almost no one cellars wine. Something north of 90 per cent of all wine purchased in the USA is consumed within 24 hours of purchase, and this number fast approaches 100 per cent if the period is extended to two weeks from purchase to consumption.'

Well, I cellar wine. I would say that I cellar a *little* wine, but Mrs K, who monitors its insidious expansion, would disagree. CJ describes it as 'a small cellar, which he maintains assiduously' – well, if keeping a cellar book, and tying little brown tags to the bottle necks to remind me of their provenance, is assiduous, then I plead guilty. And in that cellar is my Léoville-Barton 1989, which I try not to drink.

I always wanted a wine cellar. It seemed something which a

157

gentleman should possess, a simultaneous indication of taste, achievement, knowledge, *bon vivant* and generosity. My dad had a bottle of Harvey's Bristol Cream in the sideboard. My college had a wine cellar. Without the help of a printed arrow, I knew which way was up.

I was then invited for a meeting at the house of a fairly celebrated Englishman, who had just appointed me to a new job, but who had been extremely ill, and couldn't manage stairs. 'Can you nip down to the cellar and bring us up a bottle of white?' he asked me. 'Nothing too special . . . '

In those three words – 'Nothing too special . . . ' – lay an entire labyrinth of English social etiquette. The understated, throwaway remark which assumed a great deal of knowledge. The subtle declaration that, of course, he *had* a wine cellar. The implication that some of its content *was* special. And the expectation that someone he had chosen to work with knew which wines were special, but which not *too* special.

What did I bring up, everyone always asks? A sauvignon blanc. And my host smiled, and said 'That's fine.' Because, of course, he was a gentleman.

Anyway, every spring, Bordeaux makes its latest vintage wines available to buy *en primeur*. There are places better than this to find out exactly what that means – but twenty years ago now, I had decided that I needed a cellar, and this annual offer, despite my impecuniousness, was surely the place to start.

So in 1990, I bought my first ever case of serious Bordeaux, *en primeur*. It was, of course, that Léoville-Barton 1989. And thanks to my assiduousness, I have not only the invoice for this case, but the merchant's tasting notes which inspired my purchase. 'The wine represents everything that is so deservedly popular in St Julien,' they said. 'Terrific fruit encased in a firm structure, with this year an extra richness that brings more depth to the wine.'

The case – the entire case – cost me £132. There was tax and delivery to pay on top of that when it arrived, but even so we are talking about something like £160 when it was delivered eighteen months later. Bear that sum in mind.

Now, the only problem was that I had no actual cellar. I couldn't afford professional storage – and, in any case, I wanted this *spiritual* cellar, this presence of fine wine in my home. So for the next twenty years, this wooden case of claret, virtually the whole of my original 'cellar', followed the movements of my life. It was lugged between three properties, spent three years in household storage along with my furniture and four months in my sister-in-law's garage. Sadly, my 'cellar' has not always been the climate-controlled haven recommended by the experts.

And even as the years passed, the right occasion to prise open the case never arrived. Big occasions were marked with big celebrations, with too many people to share what I had. Others were marked at restaurants, or catered events, with punitive corkage charges. And was the wine actually *ready*? It never seemed the right time to start the case. And abstinence made the heart grow fonder.

Anyway, two years ago, I was invited down to my future father-in-law's for Christmas. Here was a chap, and a future brother-in-law as well, who really appreciated good wine. Earlier that year, the wine critic Tim Atkin had said in one of his last pieces for the *Guardian* that he would be drinking precisely this wine at his wedding, describing it as a 'mature, complex claret', terms which struck chords in my heart, and persuaded me that the wine must be ready to drink.

Here was an occasion on which I really wanted to appear knowledgeable, generous, etc., etc. Here were people I could share it with. Here was the special occasion for which to breach the case at last.

And it was truly gorgeous velvety claret; the bouquet rich, the tannins resolved in a soft, full flavour, great length – oh, all the things you want from old Bordeaux.

But this is *Sediment*, and there are others who write tasting notes on great wines like this; there are far more important points to make within our unique remit.

I could not drink wine of that price now. The wine that cost me £132 a case now retails for more than £80 *per bottle* – and I would wince to pay that. I didn't buy it as an investment; I bought it so that I would be able to drink wine I could not otherwise afford, which is indeed now the case. But actually it is, in those words I remember, 'too special' – and it is *not* drinking it that is really important.

My Léoville-Barton '89 is the backbone of my cellar, the wine I could serve to the grandest person who might cross my threshold. It captures and illustrates, in a single wine, all of those spiritual aspects of a cellar that I described earlier on. And it demonstrates that twenty years ago, I looked forward in life with optimism, to a point at which I have now arrived.

My assiduous cellar book contains a cutting from the *Observer*, 13 May 1990 – long before online archives – by Paul Levy, which helped persuade me into my purchase. His concluding paragraph applauds Léoville-Barton for honest pricing, and ends by praising owner Anthony Barton: '[His] reward for his integrity will come in the future, when his claret will be one of the few outstanding '89s that people can afford to drink rather than trade.'

Or, in my case, afford *not* to drink, rather than trade.

Now that my cellar is finally physically extant, it has a rolling content; I bought the 2009 vintage *en primeur* again. Perhaps some unquenchable optimism buried within me believes that there will come more occasions, in decades or two, which merit wine like this. And ultimately, that's why I cellar wine. Some say, life is too short to drink bad wine. But hopefully life is too long to simply quaff the good.

Drinking Wine
at No. 10

PK

Following my invitation for a glass of wine at 10 Downing Street . . .

No, let me start again. When I was invited to drinks with the Prime Minister . . .

I have taken yet another upward step in my social status. This is not about drinking wine at my dining table or in the study; no, this is about drinking wine behind (as the No. 10 website puts it) 'the most famous front door in the world'.

An invitation to Downing Street is understandably surrounded by security arrangements, and there are restrictions on telling people much about a visit. However, no one has told me that I cannot talk about the wine, of which I had high hopes.

Articles in the press have revealed something of the quality of the government's cellars. I thought it unlikely that they would bring out the Château Pétrus 1978, worth more than £2,500 a bottle, for our little soirée. But perhaps the Château Latour 1955, with its little note, 'Drink on v. special occasions'? This occasion was certainly v. special to *me*.

And look, the Château Palmer 1975 is described as a 'really old-fashioned style claret, rich and *excellent with some austerity*'! Precisely what we have now – some austerity! The Palmer '75 would indeed be excellent with it.

Well, needless to say, I was sorely disappointed.

There is something thrilling about arriving at Downing Street, showing your invitation to the policeman, and being guided through the gates while a gaggle of tourists look on, clearly thinking 'Who the hell is *that*?' There are various security procedures whereof I cannot speak, before you are ushered through the shiny front door and into No. 10 itself.

I must first draw particular attention to the glassware. We have had several tussles on the *Sediment* blog over appropriate drinking containers, but I can say with some confidence that No. 10 surpasses even CJ in clumsy glassware. Our wine was served in clunky, green-glass goblets, more appropriate to a campfire celebration with Robin Hood's Merrie Men.

The only possible explanation is that, along with so many other elements of such an evening, proper glassware is considered to be a security risk. These Downing Street wallahs have clearly been to a few dodgy pubs in their time; presumably, these goblets are either unbreakable, or would crumble like a car windscreen in the unlikely event of a guest attempting to 'glass' the Prime Minister.

Obviously I am not privy to the catering arrangements at No. 10. It is admittedly unlikely, even faced with yet another invasion of their Pillared Room by a group of strangers, that the Camerons simply popped down to the offie. But whether the wine was actually provided by No. 10, or chosen by our reception organisers, I do not know.

However, in standard, drinks-party manner, your goblet is proffered with a choice of red or white wine. And here's the thing. The white was Villa Maria Sauvignon Blanc, an innocuous, fruity and citrussy New Zealand wine that you can buy in virtually any supermarket or off-licence. Indeed, at the time of writing, you could get 25 per cent off at Tesco, something that might appeal more to No. 11.

Obviously we were not attending *for* the wine, but a visit to No. 10 is rather special, and this sauvignon blanc is so widely available, and so blandly drinkable, that it doesn't register as anything special whatsoever.

The same was true of the red – Campo Viejo Rioja; again, relatively innocuous, blandly drinkable and widely available. The only thing I can really say in favour of the selection of this pair is that judiciously, one is from the Commonwealth and the other from the EU; coincidence, or politics?

So basically, a lot of things are special about a drinks evening at No. 10 – but not the drinks. Perhaps they are trying to emulate the population at large by providing the kind of modestly priced, bland and unchallenging wine many people would buy for themselves. Make them feel at home. Except . . . we're not at home. We're at 10 Downing Street.

Anyway, we sipped from our health-and-safety-approved goblets, their rims thick as china mugs. There was in fact no violence, even though security had clearly overlooked the lethal potential of a weapons-grade *vol-au-vent*. The PM toured the room, meeting and greeting in an accomplished manner. A few words to the gathering; a little, probably well-used joke confusing Nick Clegg with his wife as his absent 'other half' (ho ho); and a crafted reference to the value of 'our industry' which would clearly fit any bunch of visitors.

Presumably No. 10 learnt long ago that world leaders were not averse to pocketing a reminder of their visit, and so there is absolutely nothing to, er, take home. No crested notepads, badged pencils or matchbooks. Even the gents loo air freshener and soap are, as it were, bog standard. So with no phalanx of flashbulbs to illuminate my exit, I left alone and with only my memories, into the dark of Downing Street, like a reshuffled Minister.

For a very modest outlay, you can experience the whole thing for yourself. First, down to your local retailer for a bottle of Villa Maria or Campo Viejo. Find your clunkiest heavyweight goblet, and log into the No. 10 Virtual Tour. Pick up your glass – 'Red or white, sir?' – as you view the Terracotta Room, where drinks are served; then sip your wine while viewing the Pillared Room, where guests congregate. Should you wish to avail yourself of the lavatory (surprisingly omitted from the Virtual Tour), rest assured that your own is probably not very different to the one at No. 10. This will give you the whole experience; except, of course, for the opportunity to share a few words with one of the most significant, insightful and interesting people in the country.

But if you send me an invite . . .

Dinner-Party Wine Etiquette

PK

I have always been intrigued by the etiquette of wine, the social rules and rituals that surround our drinking. And there are few occasions that contain quite so many as dinner at my father-in-law's house in Somerset.

Sometimes I feel that life is like circling an H. M. Bateman cartoon, in constant fear of committing a social *faux pas*, and being mocked as 'The man who . . . '

I spent a great deal of time myself learning about the rules that govern an English gentleman's dress. For example, I know which buttons to button on a double-breasted jacket; never to wear brown in town; and that a Brigade tie should not be worn after 6 p.m. Some of these rules are unlikely to trouble me – I am not entitled, for example, to wear a Brigade tie even *before* 6 p.m. – but one feels better for knowing them. You should know the rules before you break them.

(It was once questioned, for example, whether Edward, Duke of Windsor, then Prince of Wales, should be wearing brown suede shoes with a blue pinstripe suit. 'The Prince knows better,' said one observer, 'so it's all right.')

So naturally I am intrigued by the rules that surround the drinking of wine. Some rules, like 'red wine with meat, white wine with fish' have become so clichéd that they are featured in James Bond films, and seem to exist solely nowadays in order that wine bloggers can find clever ways to contradict them. But they are as nothing to the arcane rules that seem to govern the drinking at an English country dining table.

Dinner at my father-in-law's is not formal, but suits, ties and skirts are appreciated, albeit not on the same guest. You are expected to be 'on parade' (i.e. dressed) for drinks before dinner at 7 p.m. Sharp. Shouting upstairs to latecomers begins at about 7.02.

You must pace yourself. After the drink before dinner, there will always be a white wine to start the meal, and the inevitable port to conclude. And in between, some serious claret, often gifted by his son and myself.

On this occasion, we have ended up with three clarets to accompany the main course. My father-in-law's Tour St Bonnet 2007; my brother-in-law's Liversan 2008; and my own La Tour de By 2001. All Médoc/Haut-Médoc, all Cru Bourgeois. So, in what order should we drink them?

Well, there's a rule for that. The rule governing the order of wine service: white before red; light before heavy; young before old. It's the kind of straightforward rule all, except the most contentious, can agree makes sense. The kind of rule I like. And simple too, misunderstood only once by an elderly chap who grumbled, 'Young before old? No youngster's getting served before *me*.'

So it was white wine first, and then, on an age basis, young to old, our claret should therefore have been drunk in the order Liversan; St Bonnet; Tour de By. Easy.

However, on a light to heavy basis, it would probably be St Bonnet; Liversan; Tour de By. That order probably reflects the standing of the châteaux as well. And in either of those orders, even given our prodigious consumption, we might never have *reached* the Tour de By.

So my brother-in-law decided that the Tour St Bonnet should be kept unopened, 'as a fallback'. First *faux pas*; 'fallback' was a description he then floundered to explain to the lady on his left, who had given it to my father-in-law as a gift.

The table, properly laid of course, glitters in candlelight. But to maintain this splendid appearance, wine is served in small, beautiful crystal glasses; great at reflecting candlelight, poor at enhancing the flavour of wine. Is there a rule that the presentation of a meal is more important than its content? His son and I smuggle classic Bordeaux glasses into the dining-room, the better to appreciate the claret. This receives a baleful glare, not so much of criticism as disappointment.

After eliminating the Tour St Bonnet, young before old was, it proved, the right order. The Liversan was initially a little stern, but it softened in the decanter into a blackberry fruity, rich and earthy claret. The Tour de By was softer, denser, darker and more savoury by comparison. In this order, it was as if the latter was a fully opened version of its predecessor, an ideal sequence.

I try to request some more of it – but another rule intervenes.

It is, according to my father-in-law, vulgar to use the term 'more' wine. He will instead offer you 'a little wine?' when your glass is low. (Unless he's telling his story about Clement Attlee and Churchill's funeral, in which case he won't notice.) But he will never offer – and you must never ask – for 'more'. It's a rule that becomes increasingly hard to remember as the evening progresses, and you aim at getting through two bottles of claret, but it does add a certain Dickensian quality to the table.

As usual, the meal finishes with port, although on this occasion the decanter contains only what my father-in-law describes as 'grocer's port', i.e. Late Bottled Vintage. 'Supermarket' is never mentioned; clearly the term 'grocer' is considered disdainful enough.

Still, even with 'grocer's port', the rules prevail; the port must, as tradition demands, be passed around the table to the left. Halting my father-in-law in full declamatory flow is a rare achievement, but his granddaughter managed this by reaching across the table for the decanter. He was rendered speechless – uniquely, in my experience of a gentleman who reminds guests that 'a dinner without conversation is, literally, unspeakable'.

And, it seems, one cannot pour port for one's neighbour; one can only pour for oneself. I transgressed, assuming it was courteous to pour a glass for the lady on my left. I forgot that traditionally, of course, ladies would have left the dining room before the port was served. So this conflict of etiquettes should never have occurred; if ladies now remain in the dining room for port, one treats them as fellow gentlemen.

Why, why do we do all of this? Passing the port, not asking for more, serving wines in a particular order, pouring or not pouring . . . Why do we surround wine-drinking with arcane rules, which probably dissuade some people from even serving the stuff?

In some cases it is, genuinely, a matter of taste. That rule for the order of serving wines surely makes sense, both in terms of your palate, and in accompanying a traditionally weighted three-course meal. There may be some case for serving an old heavy red before a light young white, but if so, it's as well to know you might be expected to explain it.

In other instances, it's simply a matter of enhancing the experience. Like candlelight, it makes it *special*. The fact that we are partaking in a little shared social ritual must influence our experience of a wine, just as surely as a sight of the label. I will never know how the grocer's port might taste passed the other way, or the clarets taste in a different order; but I do know that, with all the laughter and comments about adhering to the rules, my father-in-law's dining table is an enormously enjoyable place to drink it.

And as for arcane rules, well, what else would you expect from a nation that retains peerages and royal weddings, always leaves the bottom button on a waistcoat undone, and revels in forty-two Laws of Cricket?

Drinking Wine at Lambeth Palace

PK

As I was drinking wine with the Archbishop of Canterbury . . .

You may have read my earlier piece about drinking wine with the Prime Minister at 10 Downing Street. Following that, I was able to climb even higher in the UK's Order of Precedence, having been invited to a reception at Lambeth Palace, for wine with the Archbishop of Canterbury.

Step one was to check how to address the Primate of All England. I then spent the prior evening at home practising, with a slight, deferential lowering of the head, the phrase 'Good evening, Your Grace', a phrase I am unlikely ever again to be able to utter appropriately.

(As that evening wore on, Mrs K became increasingly irritated with my other, less appropriate variations, such as 'Thank you, Your Grace', 'Yes, another glass please, Your Grace', and 'Well, if there is another sausage going, Your Grace . . . ')

Like most Londoners, I'm familiar only with the somewhat forbidding dark Tudor brick gatehouse of the Palace, on the bank of the Thames. But behind it, after name checks, etc., lies the path to the Palace itself, in a rather more collegiate yellow stone. The surrounding grounds contain gardens and apple trees, of which (as you will soon see) the Palace kitchens make use.

You pass through the Palace doorway, and realise you must be in the company of good people, because the cloakroom lacks not only an attendant, but any kind of numbering or security system. Who indeed would steal from the house of an archbishop? (Apart from a king or two . . .)

Then up a grand staircase, to where the Archbishop of Canterbury himself waited in the corridor, and welcomed each of his guests personally. This was a different tactic to that employed by the Prime Minister, who ghosted into the reception room once it was filled. I therefore got my chance to shake hands and say my cherished phrase. Sobriety at this early stage ensured that I did not say, 'Good Grace, your evening.'

And I passed on, along a corridor lined with portraits of his predecessors, to the Archbishop's reception itself, held in the Guard Room, a magnificent panelled chamber with arch-braced roof.

Unlike Downing Street, we were trusted with proper wine glasses, presumably on the basis that no one could possibly be thinking of 'glassing' the host. As opposed to glassing the Host, which would be another matter entirely. And I was delighted to see that cocktail sausages were among the canapés. Perhaps, after all, I might be grateful for having rehearsed a sausage-related remark.

The apple sauce offered alongside the sausages comes from the palace itself, a waitress explained. What about the wine, I asked? She looked at me as if I were insane. No, she said with a patient smile, I think that comes from New Zealand.

What I *meant*, of course, was to ask whether it comes from

the Archbishop's own cellar, or whether a van pulls up every once in a while purely to, er, service his guests. Because the white was indeed from New Zealand; Fairleigh Estate Sauvignon Blanc 2011. It cost £8.99 from Majestic, the wine warehouse, and given that it's produced exclusively *for* them, I think we can assume that, barring divine intervention, from thence it actually came. I stuck to the red, a perfectly palatable Australian; Oxford Landing Estates Cabernet Sauvignon and Shiraz 2010. Coincidentally this was also available via Majestic, who say that it 'goes well with Sunday roasts', a relationship to the Sabbath which may or may not boost its Church credentials.

It seemed just a little disappointing, to be in such unique circumstances, chatting with the Archbishop of Canterbury (about the poetry of T. S. Eliot, as you ask . . .) and drinking wine from somewhere as commonplace as Majestic. I mean, I shop there. *CJ* has shopped there. Like the venue and the meeting, I wish the wine could have been special and interesting too. When the occasion is unique, it's a shame the wine is everyday.

What hosting tips have I gleaned from drinking wine with these two most senior figures? Well, it seems that Rule Number One of hosting a reception with wine is that . . . you don't drink the wine. Neither of my hosts drank any of their wine. Now of course, they may be nervous of committing an inebriated *faux pas*, lunging for remaining sausages, stumbling into people and spilling wine, which would be quoted all over the newspapers next day (CRASH'N'SPLASH BANGER CLASH AT ARCHBISH BASH!).

But it may be that they know how humdrum the wine actually is at such functions. Of course, you're not *supposed* to notice or remember it. The exclusive surroundings, the speech, your one and only conversation with the host, all of those you are supposed to remember; the wine is simply lubrication. If the occasion, the host or the venue are once in a lifetime, it seems the wine can be everyday. Which is a shame for those of us who think the wine could easily be special, too.

The lesson of all this is simple. The more significant you are, the less significant the wine you can serve.

Which is why I must always serve my guests significant wine.

Port
PK

There is this *gentlemanly* thing surrounding vintage port. The great port houses were founded by English merchants, who established a unique relationship with the English aristocracy. When the ladies left a dining room, it was port which emerged to lubricate an Englishman's serious discussions. And like any English social activity, there are a whole set of rules and rituals surrounding the 'proper' drinking of port. Just the sort of historical baggage to lure someone like myself.

Indeed, we have our own historical baggage, port and I. The blame lies with a long-gone place called Champagne Charlie's, a faux-Victorian establishment on the Essex Road in the 1980s. Its artificiality was highlighted by its location on the edge of a modern housing estate, its wood panelling and sawdust floor entirely failing to disguise a construction alien to Victorian builders.

In an effort to appear historic, and recreate a kind of Falstaffian mood, Champagne Charlie's sold pints of port. *Pints*. In fact, their full quaffing experience, of which I foolishly partook in my late twenties with a friend, involved a two-pint copper jug, and two pewter pint tankards.

As a fortified wine, port actually contains within itself the very combination of wine and spirits that supposedly leads to the worse type of hangover. So I drank it with a kind of bravado, in much the same way as the Japanese eat *fugu*.

I clearly thought of myself as a successor to John 'Mad Jack' Mytton, the legendary nineteenth-century squire who could drink eight bottles of port a day, starting the first while shaving. However, what actually accompanied my own depilation next morning was the most painful, blinding headache that I have ever experienced. That morning explained to me why Norwegians refer to a hangover as *jeg har tommermenn* – 'I have carpenters in my head'.

Having decided that no, I am not Squire Mytton, nor was meant to be, I returned to a single glass after formal dinners. Port remains a stranger to my shaving routine.

But after Christmas dinner that year, I told this story as a tale of alcoholic *braggadocio*. 'A pint, eh?' said a relative, 'Well, if you like your port, I can get some rather good value vintage Kopke at the moment.' The 1983 vintage had just been declared. Kopke is the oldest of all the port houses, and vintage port seemed the sort of thing I should show an eagerness to acquire. So of course, I agreed.

A few weeks later, I was at work when he rang. 'Just to let you know,' he said, 'I've got that case of port for you.'

Case. Not a bottle, a *case*. *Twelve* bottles . . .

As someone with gentlemanly aspirations, I should have understood the quantities in which one orders one's port. The mistake was clearly mine. In which case, like a chap accidentally shooting a beater, one simply shut up, and paid up.

I wrote the cost on the case itself, to remind me – £108.68. It was a significant sum to someone in their late twenties back then. Particularly because it was invested in an entire case of port, which was not to be drunk for many years, and which would then last me for a further twelve years after that, barring an unlikely increase in the frequency of Christmas.

So began years of toting this case around. Yes, I could have paid to keep it in proper wine storage – but by now, I would have spent more in storage fees than I spent on the port (£10 a year storage sounds like nothing, until you think about storing a case for twenty-five years).

And then, a quarter-century later, it all came good. I had not only a case of seriously mature port, worth about £50 a bottle today, but had acquired more relatives who would appreciate it. Sharing your port is perhaps the best way to drink it without a hangover, since it both limits your own consumption yet multiplies the pleasure. And, dare I imagine that it imparts a certain gentlemanly quality to one's dining table? It was time to broach the case.

The bottles are sealed with hard, brittle wax – literally sealing wax – which shatters all over the option when you start to remove it. Beneath are corks that have clearly suffered over the last twenty-eight years. Some have leaked slightly, and below the first centimetre have the consistency of muesli. They disintegrate even when handled with the caution of a bomb disposal operative. But that's okay, since the sediment in vintage port requires that it's decanted. Even the label suggests it should be served with care, which makes a change from serving it with Stilton.

Some people expect vintage port to be unctuous and syrupy, like a dessert wine. In fact, this is light and pale brick-coloured. It has a raisiny bouquet, sharpened by the alcohol, and in the mouth it's rich and aromatic, a soft, dried fruit and burnt toffee flavour with enormous complexity, which resonates around the palate and nose and is immensely warming. It is *delicious*.

Why at Christmas? Well, that feels like a time for Victorian traditions. It brings a lot of people together around a dining table. And it's an *occasion*. Having gone to all this trouble, over such a long time, I shall not be opening a bottle after a TV dinner.

And I want it to last. Because, by the time of the final bottle, I may still not be a gentleman – but I will certainly be too old to go through the whole of this forty-year process again.

Claret or Bordeaux?

PK

There are many individual words that I associate with wine. My personal favourite is 'more'.

However, the word I am going to consider here is one which resonates with history, with class, with *Englishness* – it is 'claret'.

The first piece of wine knowledge that a young Englishman must acquire is that in the universities, clubs and dining rooms to which he should aspire, red Bordeaux wine is commonly called claret. He must learn this because ordering mature claret may, if he enjoys the fruits of success, become a common occurrence. But the word 'claret' is not actually *present* on the label of a good Bordeaux. It is something he is expected to *know*.

('Educated the expensive way,' sang Blur, 'He knows his claret from his Beaujolais' – not, you may note, his *Bordeaux* from his Beaujolais. Even CJ refers to red Bordeaux as claret, and he believes that a gentleman is a chap who removes the plates from a sink before he pees in it.)

Indeed, a claret which *does* describe itself as claret on its label is usually rubbish. This is because the term has been adopted as a marketing device for flogging really crap Bordeaux to

179

unsuspecting folk. The very word 'claret' conjures up Pall Mall clubs, leather armchairs and cigars, so it gets stuck on the label of grotty Bordeaux in the hope of luring *arrivistes*.

The only exception to this rule is Club Claret (or House Claret), where the character of the club (or house) is such that their selection of a Bordeaux provides an imprimatur of excellence. I can personally vouch for the Royal Automobile Club Claret and, thanks to my father-in-law, the Travellers Club Claret; whereas Supermarket Claret is virtually a contradiction in terms.

(Any St James's claret is usually perfectly acceptable, as one would expect in the cradle of gentlemen's clubs. St Francis Claret, however, is something else entirely, a good example of a wine which is *not* a claret at all. It comes from Sonoma County, California, which was not in Bordeaux the last time *I* looked. And claret is not, as their website bizarrely suggests, a varietal. We must forgive them, because they are Californian, but still.)

The very word claret, unused in France itself, is quintessentially English, and mature claret – encompassing our national love of time past – is a concept to which most English gentlemen aspire. And our main aspiration is to simply be able to afford it. For while the price of decent Bordeaux climbs ever upwards, one of the few characteristics CJ and I share with the gentry is impecuniousness.

So when a traditional English wine merchant offers a 'limited parcel of mature claret' at an absurdly affordable price, we are summoned by bells in all departments – sociological, oenological and fiscal.

There's no doubt that the wine this particular merchant was selling, Château Tour de Barbereau, has all the elements of a traditional claret. For a start, it's got the script lettering and drypoint illustration on its label which means that you feel that bit more confident putting it on a table. It's been *mis en bouteille au château*, in the Gironde, so it's not just some blend of generic Bordeaux leftovers. And it's got a year – 2006 – which could suggest maturity.

Had we but world enough and time, I could launch into a whole thing about Bordeaux vintages, but we haven't. I bought a five-year-old claret for under £6, and all we really need to know is – drinkable, or not?

Well. The nose was great: rich, and blackcurranty. That fruit came through in the mouth too, followed by a good, tannic backbone. It left that classic Bordeaux dryness on the palate as it went, and had a reasonable finish. One to sip and savour, you think.

But beware; it faded in the glass. Ultimately this was a wine without real depth, and by the end of an evening the fruits had gone and only those dry tannins really hung on. Shared amongst friends with a large glass each, great – but settle in for an evening with a bottle and a book, and a wine like this creeps quietly away from you into the night like a guilty party.

To get any wine that merits the description 'mature claret' for less than £6 is an achievement. But as we've seen, that's a term which resonates with expectations. So tell guests that 'it needs drinking up'. You will simultaneously excuse the fading glory of a lesser wine; hint at a vast and difficult-to-manage cellar; and suggest a knowledge of Bordeaux vintages. Like the difference between Bordeaux and claret, it's all in the words.

The Posh
Wine Merchants

PK

At my local posh wine merchants – the ones (like all posh wine merchants) with an ampersand in their name – facing the door, and hence visible from the street, a rack has appeared, proclaiming a selection of wines for under £10.

This is clearly designed to attract the paupers, riff-raff and ne'er-do-wells who shuffle past their door *en route* to the Tesco Express, normally pausing only to raise their eyes in longing like a labrador outside a butcher's.

An immediate giveaway of their poshness (apart from the ampersand) is the fact that they consider 'under £10' to be unusual enough to merit announcement. To put this into perspective, the website of this particular merchant offers 943 wines *above* £10. They also have wine at over £1,000 a bottle.

Their signs look as if they are written in chalk, but in fact are painted permanently. 'Good wine for under £10' one sign declares. 'Good'? As an Englishman huffily responds to most forms of advice, *I'll* be the judge of *that*.

'Change from £10 oh yeah!', which sounds like one of Paul McCartney's earlier lyrics.

And finally, 'Only got £10 no problem', which raises a couple of issues, only one of which is grammatical. If you had literally only got £10, I suspect you would have a *lot* of problems, and spending your sole remaining tenner in a wine merchant's would be way down your list of fiscal priorities.

But this particular merchant has an equally particular way of describing the wine at the upper end of their price range, too. Take the opening of their description for a bottle of 2004 Burgundy, costing £335: 'Still only just finishing its malo, so hard and gassy . . . '

'Hard and gassy'? That certainly does not encourage me to spend £335 on a bottle. It sounds like a couple of the guys at Stamford Bridge.

It's bad enough when CJ says a wine tastes of old newspapers and seems to think that's a *good* thing, but at least his wine's only £3.99.

But, hang on. 'Just finishing its malo . . . ' – what? What??

There are, presumably, people for whom the malolactic fermentation of a wine is a key purchasing influence, and for whom terms like 'needs some time', or 'not ready yet' are insufficiently specific. But it is the chatty abbreviation 'malo', which annoys me, like, yah, that's the way we banter about our £335 wine. Yah.

Anyway, in I stroll. Of course, I try to give off the air of someone who was intending to saunter all the way down the store, to the First Growth clarets and the £335 Burgundies finishing their malo at the far end, only to be rudely interrupted by the under-£10 display in my way.

Oh, what's this? Wines for under £10? Crikey! Do such things exist? How *charming*.

I am not interrupted with 'assistance' as I look at the modest selection, because obvously for £10 you're not going to get the unctuous fawning you expect when you're spending £300+ on a bottle, never mind the banter about vintages and the repartee about malolactic fermentation.

Besides, they presumably don't want to frighten away those who have been lured, nervous as sparrows, across their threshold, but are more familiar with the self-selection of the supermarket.

It's a sunny day, and I plump for an intriguing Italian white, Anima Umbra, made primarily from the Grechetto grape, which I've not encountered before. It has a couple of troublingly downmarket elements, such as gold foil on its label, which lends it a sort of bonkbuster paperback appearance; and I find when I get home that it has a green plastic cork, which is a vile and unnatural thing, resembling some kind of medical bung.

But actually, it's a thoroughly enjoyable wine. Intensely floral on the nose, lovely creamy texture, and then an extraordinary balance of full, apple and peach, fruit notes, with a crisp, refreshing aftertaste. Just the kind of acrobatics which create an excellent white to drink on its own. Yes, it *is* good wine for under £10.

Now, I'm not going to make any sweeping judgements about buying from merchants versus buying from supermarkets. But there is one fundamental difference. Clumsy as their promotional tactics may be, wines in merchants are properly priced. These are not short-term offers, with the wine doubling back up in price next week. And you can be equally confident that it's not going to be reduced next week either, to £5, or two for a tenner, or buy one get one free. This is wine which is actually *worth* £9.95.

Plus, I think it's finished its malo.

VIII

Thinking and Drinking (2)

Drinking from a Mug

CJ

I was trying to face down this Argentinian Malbec, in the right price range, screw cap, red, no vintage, all the qualities one looks for in a quality table wine; only it was proving a bit hard to get through on account of being incredibly aggressive and full of blood and sweat and heat and dust and flies and volcanic gas, and even though it was only 13.5 per cent, the thing taken as a whole had a kick like a mule and I wasn't sure how much I could swallow without blacking out. It was like drinking the floor of an abattoir. *Impasse.*

Then, in a mixture of boredom and desperation, I thought, I'll drink this out of a *mug*, that's the correct medium for this bad boy. And then I thought, I'd better try it from some other drinking vessels at the same time, to provide a comparison and get some scientific rigour into the test. So I got together my usual Duralex drinking tumbler, a Paris goblet, a nice Royal Doulton bone china teacup and a biggish coffee mug and took a hit of the Malbec from each one. The results were:

187

Duralex tumbler: Tasted the same.

Paris goblet: Tasted the same, but with an inexplicable added tweeness.

Bone china teacup: Tasted of curry. After a minor panic I decided that the tea towel I wiped it out with must have been a good bit dirtier than it looked, but either way it felt wrong, what with the deep aquamarine on white pattern and the gold edging and having to sip from it in that affected tea-drinking way.

Mug: Tasted just right. We're talking about a proper 250ml glazed earthenware mug here, with a full builder's handle, software-maker's logo printed on it, the whole thing thick and robust enough to survive being dropped repeatedly on the kitchen floor. When I mentioned this to PK he got incredibly exercised, as ever; turns out he has different mugs for different times of the day, some for tea some for coffee, some china some porcelain. *Thickness of rim*, he kept insisting. Well, this had a rim as thick as my small toe and all the better for it. The filthy Malbec sat at the bottom, still belligerent but knowing when it was beaten, and every *quaff* only made it taste better.

Picture my excitement at discovering a new way to interpret a familiar drinking experience. Feeling bullied by your rough red wine? Drink it from a mug! With a mug, *you* are in charge, *you* call the shots, *you* get a Hemingwayesque sensation as if you were a partisan up in the mountains, rudely slaking your thirst before a) wenching b) killing Fascists.

On the other hand: if I do start drinking wine from a mug on a regular basis, it's going to look like a piece of willed and slightly pathetic eccentricity. I have no beard, nor do I speak Catalan. At the same time, no one will ever tear me away from my beloved Duralex tumbler, except possibly to give me a larger one.

But then again, this business of drinking wine from a glass: it's a relatively recent practice, after all, since mass-produced wine glasses only got going from around the very end of the nineteenth century. Before that, glassware was for the gentility; the rest of us drank out of anything that didn't leak. It's not a given. And the mug was and is *good*, satisfying and apt and with an extra safety margin provided by the handle. Its only drawback, in fact, is that you can't see how much wine is left except by peering down inside, and that only gives you a very approximate sense. Maybe one of those transparent measures built into the wall of the mug, like you get in electric kettles, would do the job.

It needs further thought. *Txin Txin.*

Nostalgia – Le Piat d'Or

PK

When L. P. Hartley described the past as another country, where they do things differently, he was almost right. The past is another *county*, and that county is Cumbria.

In many respects, the Lake District *is* the past. A place with sweetshops. A place with milk in bottles. A place where the local hardware shop offers a selection – a selection, mind you – of replacement walking-stick ferrules. And a place where, on a recent familial visit, I found a bottle of Piat d'Or.

There is something irresistible about brands from our past, about Spangles and Mateus Rosé, Angel Delight and Tiffin bars. Is it that we want to see if things remain the same? Is it that we want to test them against our now more experienced, grown-up palates? Or is it the simple lure of nostalgia, what *Mad Men*'s Don Draper described as 'a twinge in your heart, far more powerful than memory alone'?

Wine-drinking in the UK was built upon brands like Piat d'Or and Hirondelle, which have largely disappeared from winesellers in the capital. When customers were frightened of varieties and vintages, they were reassured by slogans like '*It's about as likely as a duff bottle of Hirondelle*'.

Some of these brands, particularly whites, are forever being 'relaunched' for the new, wine-literate market. I tried for some time last summer to find a bottle of a supposedly 'relaunched' Blue Nun, but I mistakenly purchased the relaunch *before* last, far too sugary for my palate and which left my teeth feeling carpeted.

So there was a certain element of nostalgic excitement in discovering that, in the Lake District at least, you can still buy a bottle of Piat d'Or red for just £4.95.

Sadly, this is not quite the Piat d'Or of our youth. Launched in 1978, it went through its own 'relaunch' in 2001. Despite its French name, and an ad campaign which insisted that '*The French adore le Piat d'Or*', the French had actually never heard of the stuff. So in 2001, it was decided that the whole French connection should be abandoned. 'France and the French are no longer aspirational,' said their marketing manager at the time, which will come as news to those big buyers of Bordeaux in China and Hong Kong today.

How French is Piat d'Or, anyway? It does declare it is *produit de France*, but the label also reveals it is actually bottled in Italy. And its description is printed in English, French and *German*, a rare opportunity these days to see these three European cultures in accord on a document.

The 'rebranded' Piat d'Or declares its grape variety – Merlot, in my case – which is just as well, because you certainly couldn't identify it from its taste. Initially it has a strong blackcurranty nose, but like that first fragrant opening of a jar of instant coffee, this is utterly misleading. The bouquet, and indeed any taste of fruit, vanishes pronto, leaving me only a nasty, brackish aftertaste from the alcohol.

But there was something reassuring about finding it at all. The rest of the country may have moved on, but as with a display of walking-stick ferrules, the presence of Piat d'Or may reflect the comforting refusal of Lake District retailing to discard the attitudes of the past.

Indeed, one of my family asked if there was any chance of the local supermarket's wine buyer getting in some Cloudy Bay? No, he said, demonstrating a profound misunderstanding of the whole idea of modern retailing. 'There's no point. It sells out as soon as we get it in.'

Celebrity Wines – the
Sediment Selection

CJ

In a desperate attempt to make some money, I have decided to get into the online celebrity wine retailing business. And no, this has nothing to do with the Francis Ford Coppola range, or the Ernie Els range, or (tragically) the AC/DC range, or indeed anything that might actually involve growing grapes or making wine or getting anyone's consent. No, the idea came to me, like the smell coming off a rubbish tip in July, to take the cheapest wholesale grog I could find and simply append any name to it which has a slightly wine-flavoured quality – to the credulous, inattentive and hard of hearing, at least – and at once quadruple the throughput of interested parties to the retail website.

How does it work? You ask. Well, for example:

Mel Blanc: a dry white, made of absolutely anything (Pinot Gris, Sauvignon Blanc, Chenin Blanc) as long as it embodies the cheeky comedic brilliance of the late Mel Blanc, *the Man of a Thousand Voices* – among them Bugs Bunny, Daffy Duck and Barney Rubble. A fun-loving, often hilarious wine, bright, with a subtle nose and a crisp finish, perfect served chilled as an apéritif, or just to while away those balmy summer evenings. Online price: £5.99 a bottle, or £4.99 if you buy more than two.

Robert Graves 2010: another white, but a very different beast from the Mel Blanc. This comes from the workbench of Luc Grenouille – one of the Bordeaux region's most exciting new wine makers – a classic yet modern Graves, dense with peachy overtones and grassy undertones, a fine wine to accompany a reading of *I, Claudius* or *The White Goddess*, but not, on balance, *Goodbye to All That*. Complex, occasionally unsettling, the Robert Graves 2010 is a wine that will get people talking. Online price: £10.99 a bottle, or £11.99 if you buy a case, as the cardboard's surprisingly expensive.

Nick Cave: a selection of thunderous, doom-laden reds (Cabernet Sauvignon, Malbec, Shiraz, mainly) and grinding, industrial whites (mostly Sauvignon Blanc, some paraffin) from this Australian cellar, which has been turning out spectacular wines for over thirty years. The Nick Cave range is not for the faint-hearted, nor for the inexperienced. Mature drinkers, though, will find much to enjoy in these wines, ranging from £1.99 to £199.99 a bottle, all presented in uniformly unlabelled black glassware. Not to be confused with Nicolas Cava, a different drink altogether.

Merle Oberon: a tribute to the lovely, late, movie actress, this soft, velvety Merlot, with keynotes of berries and plums, is made from grapes grown all over the world – a gesture to the international, jet-setting, sometimes tragic, lifestyle of the star of such classics as *Aren't We All?*, *First Comes Courage* and *All Is Possible in Granada*. It's an easy-drinking, quietly glamorous red, with a picture of Miss Oberon as Lady Blakeney from *The Scarlet Pimpernel*, on the label. Best enjoyed at room temperature, with one's hair in a chignon. Online price: £7.99 a bottle.

Vin Diesel: a range of reds, white and rosés specifically aimed at the younger, blockbuster movie crowd. Any one of the Vins Diesel will be certain to delight, stimulate and intoxicate its consumer, leaving his or her ears ringing and with a head like a cement block. No-nonsense, semi-automatic, take-no-prisoners reds are Shiraz with 10 per cent Mourvèdre; no-nonsense, semi-automatic, take-no-prisoners whites are Pinot Gris with 10 per cent Viognier; no-nonsense, semi-automatic, take-no-prisoners rosés are dilute Red Bull with 20 per cent antifreeze. Online price: £4.99 a bottle, £3.99 by the case. The safety catch is off with these bad boys! (Proof of age required.)

You get it? In the confusion that invariably attends buying anything online, I can thus simultaneously befuddle authentic wine purchasers, *littérateurs*, movie buffs *and* music fans into paying for something they neither need nor want, merely by making my assets work harder. It can't fail.

Wine and Game

PK

'Goes well with game' – how often do you read that about a wine? But how often do you actually *eat* game? *Exactly*.

Most people are ignorant of game. There are many for whom a partridge will only ever be a bird that spends its Christmas in a pear tree.

But wine merchants clearly think that, by associating a wine with game, they are somehow imbuing that wine with posh, aristocratic qualities – qualities that would not accrue from an association with, say, sausages. Suddenly, they think, that wine will appeal to people who like to imagine themselves going out on a Downton Abbey shooting party. They may not actually eat game, or even know how it tastes – but they will buy a wine which they believe might, on some stately dining table, accompany it.

Such people might visit a merchant like Berry Bros & Rudd, who, with their royal appointments, are probably the most aristocratic of wine merchants. And if you don't feel you have the status to enter their St James's premises, there is always their website. This is clearly the place to go if you're looking for wine to accompany game; just search various possible main courses, and see how many wines come up. On the day I did this it suggested: beef 22 wines, fish 52, lamb 27, pork 9 and game . . . 53.

Do the aristocracy need twice as many recommendations for game suppers as they do for beef or lamb? To meet that level of consumption, they'd have to be taking to the moors with sub-machine guns.

Or take Majestic, a merchant surely more representative of the wider UK wine-buying public. Their search facility paired some 45 wines with lamb, 43 with fish and 17 with sausages. But they also paired 16 wines with game. Do Majestic customers really need as many wines to match game as they do to match sausages?

Majestic seem strangely all inclusive about the style of wine which actually *pairs* with game. Because according to their own style descriptions, the wines they recommended are either: medium-bodied (6); rich, spicy (5); light, elegant (3); full and fruity (1); or powerful (1). You might just as well pick a wine blindfolded.

In any case, what is this blanket term, 'game'? Game ranges from the delicate flavour of partridge, through the richness of venison and the darkness of hare to, say, snipe, a bird whose flavour is described as 'a woody flavour similar to sweetly rotting wild mushrooms'. (That description is from Rules, a historic London restaurant which I adore for its game, but which from this depiction clearly has problems understanding the notion of 'appetising'– at least to me.) There are too many wines, of too great a variety, being recommended to pair with game, for it to be anything other than a marketing exercise. Which is really a pain, when you actually do want a wine to go with game.

Which I did. Because I was cooking a supper of pheasant breasts. Now, I realise, because of the aforementioned associations, that this will only fuel CJ's notion that I am some aspirational Lord Snooty. But in fact this was wire-basketed from Sainsbury's supermarket, at a meagre £4 for two. Pheasant like this lies somewhere between the texture of pork and the taste of chicken, and is quite mild in flavour. (Remember that traditionally, game is hung for a week or so to decompose and give it that 'gamey' flavour; in Sainsbury's meat department, decomposition is not actively encouraged.)

Now, happy as I am to display my skills at plating up – are you watching, *Masterchef?* – I could not begin to pretend that this is an inherently aristocratic meal. Believe me, I am not wearing white tie. Not even black tie. Not even a *tie*. The closest my supper got to a shooting party is the rogue piece of lead shot I found within it, which almost cracked a tooth.

So I thought I should pair it with a wine which (a) claimed on its back label to go with game, but which (b) an aristo would not touch with a shooting stick. Or, for that matter, his woodcock.

Les Garrigues Carignan 2010 is a wine from the Mont Tauch co-operative in the Languedoc, rapidly becoming a handy imprimatur for decent cheaper wines. This wine would be unlikely to find its way onto a stately dining table. Carignan is a grape historically associated with table and country wines; unlikely to appeal to an aristo trying to impress his chums. Especially when the wine comes from a co-operative, which sounds dashed close to Communism. And most old-school toffs want their chummies to think they paid more than a tenner for their vino, so even if it's not terribly good, they tend towards tried and trusted B&B – Bordeaux and Burgundy.

No, this wine is more appropriate for those of you who think 'beaters' are chaps who drink Stella.

Les Garrigues is all right with my fresh, supermarket pheasant, but definitely lacks the weight I would want to accompany serious game. For £8.75 it's nothing special – and isn't game supposed to be special?

So don't believe the merchants. There is nothing inherently posh about wine that goes well with game. It's a pretty arcane pairing, given the small amounts of game people actually consume, and pretty pointless, given the variety of game itself. It is a description simply trading upon our notion of class.

Which may, in itself, be misplaced. Peter Jay once memorably wrote in *Oxford Today*, 'As for the aristocracy, are they not better left where P. G. Wodehouse safely bestowed them, as objects of derision?'

And as for me, I shall return to a social position in which snipe and grouse are merely descriptions of my behaviour.

Nostalgia – Wine Drinking
with Mary Quant
CJ

In a fit of helpless nostalgia-seeking, I find a pile of colour magazines from the early 1970s and churn through them looking for whatever past I think I might have to thank for my current condition. The contents are intrinsically complex, the early decade riddled with a nostalgia of its own as the bright promise of the 1960s turns out to be a bit crappier than anyone had anticipated, leading to an enthusiastic rediscovery of earlier styles (Victoriana, Deco, nineteenth-century sideburns, Regency high-waisted skirts) to take away the taste of the present.

But also much simpler, in that the hydra-headed monster of consumer choice is still relatively under control: which means that the stuff in the adverts between the articles, the stuff you can buy with your rapidly depreciating currency (inflation hovering around 10 per cent per annum in the UK, rocketing to over 24 per cent in '75) enjoys a much-reduced taxonomic range, and doesn't have much going for it when you do buy it. A trawl through the ads is therefore blissfully underwhelming. A new Ford Granada gives you a push-button radio with speakers front and rear! Warerite offers a better range of standard sheet sizes than any other laminate manufacturer! And if you want some wine with your food? Blue Nun, from Sichel: *Right through the meal.* Not just one less thing to worry about, twenty less things. Forty!

If Blue Nun doesn't do it for you, Deinhard Green Label ('a crisp, refreshing wine characteristic of the finest Moselles') should provide adequate cover, as will Goldener Oktober ('cool, clear, light-hearted'), or Deinhard Hanns Christof ('a smooth, well-balanced hock'), or for red, Bull's Blood ('full-bodied'), or for sparkling, Asti Martini ('a wine with finesse and perfect balance'), or, indeed, Marimont ('the light, delicate, sparkling wine from France'), at a very reasonable £1.20 a bottle. Top and tail it with a Harvey's Bristol Cream ('the best sherry in the world') and a Cockburn's Special Reserve ('a very fine bottle of port') and you're away. Quite apart from which, you're probably smoking so much (did *everyone* smoke in the Seventies? Judging by the pictures, then, *yes*), any subtleties in the drink are going to be as evanescent as starlight reflected in a puddle. Life couldn't be simpler.

Except: a little cloud, like a man's hand, in the form of an advert from Mary Quant – of all people, the famous fashion designer – who, in 1974, is running her own wine import business, Mary Quant (Wine Shippers) of Ives Street, Chelsea. And she is going to shatter the conventions of mainstream English wine drinking by bringing us a properly sourced Côtes du Rhône ('famed for its rich, full red wines'), a respectable Blanc de Blancs and (something for the ladies, no doubt) a Bordeaux Demi-Sec, all on mail order. 'Appellation Contrôlée wine for around £1 a bottle,' she announces, and while part of me leaps up at the chance to get away from the Deinhard Hanns

Christof being boosted as if it were a '49 Margaux, the rest of me sees, for all Ms Quant's admirable high-mindedness, the dawn of the beginning of the Modern Age, with its domesticated wine snobbery, its specialisms, its drudgery of choice.

The nostalgia trail ends here, in fact, with Mary Quant, not least because of what I am about to drink when I finally put away this stash of yellowing old colour supplements and fashion magazines: that chi-chi Waitrose Grenache – not bad, a nice mix of, frankly, fresh squid and fireworks in the nose – but am I getting any more real pleasure, real quality-of-life pleasure, than if I were necking a bottle of Goldener Oktober and considering myself rather a swell for doing so? Exactly.

And if that makes me sound like an old man who yearns to grow a pair of scimitar-shaped sideburns and drive around in a Ford Granada with a beige vinyl roof while smoking a Rothmans King Size, well, I'm not going to say it ain't so.

Drinking Wine
Like James Bond

PK

James Bond was originally not that much of a wine drinker. Spirits, cocktails, yes; the ubiquitous Martini, and of course champagne – but the writer Cyril Ray, who worked with Bond's creator Ian Fleming, once said that Fleming 'knew nothing about wine except what he was told when he rang up friends in the wine trade, and then usually got it wrong'.

Perhaps that's why in both books and films Bond stuck primarily to the irreproachable Château Mouton-Rothschild. He drank a 1947 with Goldfinger; half a bottle while *On Her Majesty's Secret Service*; a 1934 ordered by M in *Moonraker*; and a '55 in *Diamonds Are Forever* – where, of course, Bond unveiled the assassin Wint because the man didn't know that Mouton-Rothschild is a claret. And, fitting to the perpetrator of such a crime, killed him. (Frankly, for using a gas ejector to open the bottle, he deserved to be shot.)

But recently, the American author Jeffery Deaver wrote a new James Bond novel, *Carte Blanche*. And appropriately, just as the 1950s Bond knew all about cocktails, Deaver's contemporary Bond is something of a wine connoisseur. The question is whether the wines he enjoys today fit the James Bond we have always aspired to be. After all, like most English men of a certain age, I have always felt something of the Bond about myself . . .

In *Carte Blanche*, Bond is invited to lunch at the Travellers Club on Pall Mall, by 'a solid man in his mid-sixties, identified only as the "Admiral"'. (He later turns out to have been M.) Deaver has certainly got the right venue for such a diplomatic assignation, and thanks to my father-in-law I can vouch for the descriptions of both the club and its typical member. But the wine?

Menus descended. Bond ordered halibut on the bone, steamed, with Hollandaise, boiled potatoes and grilled asparagus. The Admiral selected the grilled kidney and bacon, then asked Bond, 'Wine?'

'Yes, please.'

'You choose.'

'Burgundy, I should think,' Bond said. 'Côte de Beaune? Or a Chablis?'

'The Alex Gambal Puligny, perhaps?' the waiter suggested.

'Perfect.'

Fools! It should be Puligny-*Montrachet* – no one who knew their Burgundy would omit the legendary suffix. Bond would surely delight in correcting the waiter, know that both of the two 't's are silent, and suavely order it from him properly. Then kill him.

Except, he wouldn't order it. Not just because it's a poor

pairing with grilled kidney and bacon. Nor because it has an ugly modern label. But because it's not on the wine list at the Travellers Club. Indeed, I was told, 'Regarding the wine, I'm afraid no one ever heard of it being served in the club house.'

So that's the end of that one. James Bond would not be drinking that particular wine at the Travellers, and so nor shall I. (Although, if you are ever in the fortunate position yourself of ordering a white Burgundy at the Travellers, I would have suggested the Meursault 2002 Cuvée Tete de Murger, Domaine Patrick Javillier, whose flavour has been rather poetically described as 'haunting' . . .)

Bond eventually heads off to South Africa to pursue the usual shenanigans – which, as he wines and dines a female executive, start with an order of a Rustenberg Peter Barlow Cabernet 2005.

This is a Bordeaux-style red, possibly a little young, but given all the government cutbacks, an understandable substitute for someone whose expense account can surely no longer bear the cost of Mouton-Rothschild.

However, going from one extreme to the other, I think we have to ask whether James Bond would order a wine which was sold in Tesco. Last seen in a wire basket alongside a special offer meat pie for one? Is that going to impress the woman he is trying to seduce? Though that outcome is never really in doubt, given that her name is Felicity Willing . . .

Willing by name and, as it proves, by nature. And she is responsible for the third of the wines he supposedly enjoys. When she later visits him for a return match, as it were, 'a wine bottle appeared from her shoulder bag – vintage Three Cape Ladies, a red blend from Muldersvlei on the Cape. Bond knew its reputation. He took out the cork and poured.' (Good to see he's mastered that tricky sequence!) 'They sat on the sofa and sipped. "Wonderful," he said.'

This wine proved extremely difficult to buy in London by the bottle; I have to thank the enormously helpful Handford Wines on the Old Brompton Road, a lovely, traditional wine merchant whose knowledge, service and sheer Englishness would surely have merited Bond's own custom.

Bond's 'wonderful' is not the most precise tasting note I have come across. Nor is it, in this case, the most accurate. This is an immensely muscular wine, dark purple in colour with a hot, foresty bouquet. Perhaps it's been whacked around its privates with a knotted rope.

It's dense, almost cloying in the mouth, dominated by Cabernet Sauvignon but with just a little edge from Pinotage and Syrah in the blend, and a long, echoing finish. And it's so heavy and powerful, with 14.5 per cent alcohol, it really needs food to carry it down. It has the lumbering strength of *Moonraker*'s villain Jaws, rather than the finesse of Bond himself.

Bear in mind that this wine is *not*, as its overexcited PRs suggest, Bond's own choice of seduction wine, but his Willing partner's. Nevertheless, Bond deems it 'wonderful', and like him it is ruthlessly effective. Shortly after sipping it, 'He kissed her and slowly began to undo the buttons . . . ' I'm sure Handford Wines will help anyone wishing to recreate at least the sipping part of this scene.

So 007 could not have savoured the 'Puligny' as described. The Rustenberg Peter Barlow is certainly appropriate in both taste and looks (nice traditional label), but may be too commonplace. Bond finds Three Cape Ladies more 'wonderful' than I, but it certainly proves seductive. Hmmm.

Bond's own London club, Blades, has a knowledgeable wine waiter in Grimley. Faced with a choice of wines in *Moonraker*, Bond says 'Perhaps I could leave it to Grimley?'

Yes, perhaps he should.

POSTSCRIPT:

After this post appeared, Jeffery Deaver himself contacted *Sediment*. 'Yes,' he remarked, 'a bit shocking that some of the things in a Bond novel would never happen in real life, eh?! Luckily, my wonderful readers grant me a literary licence so that I can entertain them a bit.'

Nostalgia – Regency Drinking

CJ

It happens like this. I cautiously pour out another glass of special offer Romanian Pinot Grigio, hoping the wife hasn't been keeping count, when she says, 'Did you start that bottle this evening?'

'I certainly did not,' I reply, jumping a bit and slopping some of the precious grog over the side of the glass. 'It's been around for a couple of days.' The imputation is clear, though, that even if it *has* been around for a couple of days, the contents, so far as she is concerned, are going down too fast. I, naturally, reckon otherwise, and actually start rehearsing a self-serving little speech in my head about drinking at the end of the eighteenth and start of the nineteenth centuries, in order to make my position clear.

'You do realise,' I say to myself, 'that whatever you may think of *my* drinking habits, William Pitt the Younger (1759–1806) was famous for his ability to get through six bottles of port a day and remain functional, and one or two heroically constituted drinkers of that period were believed to manage twice that much. Yes, the bottles were smaller than today's – nearer half a litre than three-quarters – and the alcohol content of Regency era port was lower than today's stuff; more like that of a hefty modern table-wine. And after all, you couldn't drink the water, and tea was for ladies. But the quantities were still huge, infinitely more than I could ever manage. *And* you started first thing in the morning, you didn't wait like a slavering dog for six o'clock at night.

'Breakfast,' I continue, wordlessly, 'for even a relatively self-denying drinker might be accompanied by claret or ale, or perhaps a hock and seltzer to settle the stomach. A glass of sherry or Madeira was taken in the middle of the morning, any outdoor activities would require a brandy bottle along the way, and then, by five in the evening, the champagne would come out. And that would be followed by other types of wine, port, brandy, and possibly more champagne to round the day off. French wines (other than champagne) were often frowned upon as being too prissy for the determined English drinker – quite apart from being increasingly difficult to come by as the wars (Revolutionary/Napoleonic) with France dragged on and the stuff had to be smuggled across the Channel. Iberian wines – port, Madeira, sherry – were much more to this nation's robust tastes.

'Those on reduced budgets or with unscrupulous wine merchants,' I also observe inwardly and no longer quite to the point, 'were quite likely to find that their "old port" had been artificially generated by adding supertartrate of potash to some immature slop; and that their fine wines were routinely acquiring a nuttier flavour thanks to bitter almonds, which contained prussic acid. Still,' I note, coming back into focus, 'it didn't stop the drinking. Apparently, Pitt the Younger and his pal, Henry Dundas (later Lord Melville), turned up at the Commons just at the outbreak of war in 1793, pissed as whelks, giving rise to this humorous couplet:

'I cannot see the Speaker, Hal, can you?
'What! Cannot see the Speaker, I see two!'

'*Everybody* drank,' I conclude silently but with increasing self-righteousness, 'even Jane Austen, who, when staying with smart relatives at Godmersham in Kent, wrote, in 1813, *I am put on the sofa near the fire, and can drink as much wine as I like.* The sainted Jane Austen, this is, clearly determined to get outside a bottle before anyone came round and started asking *her* what her consumption was likely to be for the day. It wasn't until the arrival of the Victorians with their monomaniacal prudery that all this had to come to an end, and . . . '

I realise that the wife has got her back turned to me. The interior monologue stops. I swiftly pour another glassful and then make great play of screwing the cap tightly back on the bottle, just so she can see.

I did, of course, start the bottle this evening.

Unfinished Bottles
PK

How have I managed to end up with five half-finished bottles of wine dotted about my abode?

They are piling up, in the manner of half-read books, which might or might not get finished. Like half-used pots of paint, which might or might not get used. I haven't finished the last one, but I've started a new one – in the way that one used to have an increasing stack of half-recorded VCR cassettes.

Pumped out beneath their Vac-U-Vin bungs, they sit around, slowly deteriorating, like their owner. And if I'm going to be spotted by Mrs K opening a sixth, I had better have a damned good explanation.

So let me explain.

Bottle One. This was the bog-standard bottle of red which I opened several days ago, to accompany an equally bog-standard supper. The description 'bog-standard' is not necessarily critical; it simply means that I cooked it (not Mrs K), and for myself alone (not Mrs K), and so the cooking techniques employed are likely to be less *sous-vide*, more boil-in-bag. Nor are my 'bog-standard' dishes likely to be found in most pairing notes, which as I have observed before seem more interested in ocelot and abalone than toad in the hole. So a 'bog-standard' bottle of red then, half of which nicely accompanied a solo supper.

Two. The bottle of white that I had to open the following night, because we were eating fish. Obviously I can't expect our suppers to be dictated by the bottle of wine I happened to open the night before – can I? Our supper cuisine veers across the globe like the Olympic opening parade ('Iraq! . . . Ireland! . . . Israel! . . . Italy! . . . ') Yet some aspects of our household diet, like the relentless presence of varieties of green vegetables, remain as repetitive as a Steve Reich composition. If we similarly narrowed our diet down to variations on red meat alone, it would make my wine selection 50 per cent easier.

But no; like a recalcitrant schoolboy, I accept the need to rotate fish, fowl and indeed neither. The previous night's red was put on hold, rather than smother a nice piece of hake beneath a duvet of Monastrell. So there's now an unfinished bottle of white as well.

Three. This is the Shiraz that tasted so unbelievably foul that I couldn't get beyond the first mouthful. Generously, I assume that it was corked or something, and not that there was a carcass in the fermentation plant. Having bought this bottle in an offer I of course have a second bottle of the stuff, being the only way of getting it at the reduced (i.e. proper) price. So I thought somehow that I would keep this one to see if the second was as bad. If it was, then I would take both of them back. But because the first bottle was *so* vile, I haven't had the nerve to open and taste the second yet. So the first is just festering there, like gangrene in a bottle.

Four. This was the rather nice red I once planned to write about. The problem is, it was so nice that Mrs K and I between us polished off, ooh, three-quarters of the bottle – and a quarter of a bottle is nowhere near sufficient to go with a meal. Even if I bring it out with the line, 'You're not drinking tonight, are you?' – always a dangerous gambit – there won't even be enough for me alone. There's an argument that a small glass of really nice wine can cause more mental anguish than half a bottle of bad.

So basically, bottle four is waiting in case I get round to writing about it, following an occasion on which I am drinking at home alone, and willing to settle for just one smallish glass of wine. Which isn't really going to happen . . .

Five. This is half a bottle of dessert wine – because, with the best will in the world (and that was mine), the guests at my birthday dinner who were not driving and who were still drinking by the time of the dessert only consumed the *other* half a bottle of dessert wine between them.

It would be preposterous to start drinking dessert wine each evening with the kind of plebeian puddings that emerge from our freezer. Mrs K rarely eats desserts, so I am left alone with various paltry combinations of ice cream, yoghurt, fruit and nuts; none of which remotely justify the quality, cost, or indeed the risk of a flooded suitcase, attached to a Pedro Ximénez I determinedly brought back in my luggage from Seville. So there it sits, awaiting another grand occasion with guests. By which time it will probably be undrinkable . . .

Six. This is the red I just opened to have with supper. Because bottle 1) is now so old, it's better left for cooking; 2) is white, and is also now so old it's better left for cooking; 3) is undrinkable; 4) doesn't quite have enough in it for a meal; and 5) is only for grand desserts.

Inevitably, we will only drink half of bottle 6.

So tomorrow will find me plaintively wailing: why have I got *six* half-finished bottles of wine in my abode?

213